...companies with highly engaged employees generated financial outcomes that were far superior...

If management cannot convince their own people of the merits of their corporate strategy without resorting to threats and intimidation, then they may as well give up and go home. After all, if the employees responsible for putting the plan into action neither understand it nor support it, then there is virtually no chance of successful execution. And the discord generated by senior management's combative approach is certain to lower staff morale.

This is where employee engagement enters the picture. The measurement industry that has sprung up around this subject has generated overwhelming evidence *(see Chapter 2 for details)* of the damage these tyrannical executives are inflicting on their organisation's bottom line.

For example, a Towers Perrin-ISR study found that companies with highly engaged employees generated financial outcomes that were far superior to those delivered by companies whose employees exhibited signs of low engagement.[5] The numbers are startling. Looking at the performance of the two groups over a 12-month period reveals a 52 per cent difference between their rate of operating income growth and a 39 per cent difference between their rate of earnings per share growth. With figures like these hitting the headlines, it's becoming harder for executives to argue that a top-down, *'command-and-control'* approach is the only way to deliver the results the market demands.

Management teams that continue to ignore this evidence and the clear message it sends will eventually learn, at a cost to their shareholders, that their outdated approach

Leaders who are setting out to lift their organisation's engagement scores do not have a single, clear-cut path to follow.

to managing human capital is a drag on workplace productivity and profitability. The threat to their organisation's financial performance may not be apparent in this year's, or even next year's results, but the warning signs are there and include: declining employee satisfaction and commitment levels, falling customer satisfaction and advocacy scores and shrinking market share and margins.

Mercifully, an increasing number of management teams have seen the writing on the wall and are beginning to alter their approach. Every week the newspapers identify yet another financial institution, resource company or retailer that has taken the plunge and commenced a program aimed at lifting their employees' engagement levels.

The new mantra is: happy staff, happy customers, happy shareholders. Advocates of this *'people-first'* approach, including Gail Kelly the recently appointed CEO of Westpac Banking Corporation, see it as an important part of their strategic armoury. As she explained during her time at the helm of St George Bank: "Using our strategic framework we have developed a simple formula for success. Through engaged people delivering great customer experiences to our target customers we will be able to deliver consistently superior financial results for our shareholders."[6]

This, of course, is much easier said than done. It is an enormous challenge to create an operating environment that persuades employees to intellectually and emotionally commit to the vision, buy-in to the corporate strategy and operate in alignment with the organisation's values.

Leadership teams cannot approach this job half-heartedly. To succeed, they need to develop and deploy an employee engagement strategy that touches everyone and everything within their organisation. But where should these teams start if they want to lift the level of engagement inside their business? What's the first step they should take, and the second, and the one after that? Where's the finish line? How long will it take to reach that line? And perhaps most importantly, how much will it cost?

These are all valid questions, to which there are no straightforward answers. Leaders who are setting out to lift their organisation's engagement scores do not have a single, clear-cut path to follow. They need to take their business on its own unique engagement journey, plotting and adjusting their course according to the prevailing conditions. On the bright side, those pioneering companies who set out on their journey a few years back now have the quantifiable evidence to prove that this is a voyage worth taking.

CHAPTER 2

Making the Case for Employee Engagement

Only a few years ago, the only thing senior executives were able to measure was their employees' satisfaction level, a metric that had little or no connection to business performance. This left management in a fix. Human behaviour has never been the easiest of things to calibrate and without a set of numbers to guide them many executives felt unable to tackle their mounting *people and culture* problems.

Opportunely, the emergence of the trend towards conducting staff engagement surveys has heralded a new era in the measurement and management of workforce performance. Thanks to the efforts of research organisations like Hewitt Associates, the Gallup Organization, Hays, TNS and Towers Perrin-ISR, leadership teams now have access to research tools that quantify the previously hard to define subjects of employee commitment and motivation.

These tools have enabled executives to identify and examine the links between employee engagement and financial performance. What they have discovered has helped them to grasp the connection between good people practices and the bottom line.

Some of the figures touted by the research companies are jaw-dropping, and even the most cynical of executives struggle to dismiss them. For example, a recent Hewitt Associates study revealed staff engagement levels are 20 per cent higher at double-digit profit growth companies than those at single-digit growth companies.[7] Similarly, a Towers Perrin-ISR study found firms with highly engaged employees achieved a 13.2 per cent improvement in net income growth, while those firms with low employee engagement

Some of the figures touted by the research companies are jaw-dropping, and even the most cynical of executives struggle to dismiss them.

levels experienced a decline of 3.8 per cent over the same period.[8] Further, an examination of shareholder returns by Watson Wyatt found that companies with highly committed employees delivered a 112 per cent total return to their shareholders over a three-year period, compared to a 76 per cent return delivered by those companies whose employees exhibited low commitment levels.[9] These numbers seemingly confirm the existence of a link between high levels of employee engagement and superior business performance.

However, while these retrospective analyses provide a certain form of reassurance, they also leave an impression that engagement is a black art. The numbers are impressive, but how did the companies actually achieve these improvements? Is the connection between engagement and performance as strong as the figures suggest?

Helpfully, a growing number of companies who have achieved success in this area have shared their stories. Perhaps the most well-known case study is that of the American retailer Sears, Roebuck and Company. In a landmark Harvard Business Review article, three members of the Sears' management team explained how the development of an employee-customer-profit chain helped transform the performance of this moribund business.[10] The authors recount how the leadership team spent three years developing and fine-tuning a model that linked management behaviour to employee attitudes, employee attitudes to customer satisfaction and customer satisfaction to financial performance.

Sears' internal model revealed that a 5 point improvement in employee attitude led to a 1.3 point improvement in customer satisfaction, which in turn drove a 0.5 per cent

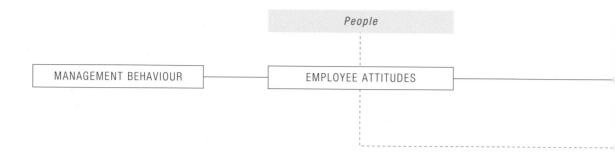

increase in revenue growth. It's a persuasive case history and the numbers certainly stack up. An increase of US$250 million in Sears' market capitalisation is attributed to the additional revenue derived from the deployment of the program.

Closer to home, the performance of the Australia and New Zealand Banking Group (ANZ) provides further evidence of the link between employee engagement and superior business performance. In a recent Hewitt Best Employers Study, ANZ achieved an engagement score of 64 per cent, which placed it ahead of its peers and 6 percentage points above the benchmark for Australian financial services organisations.[11] Building on this theme, a recent Nielsen Retail Banking Report looked at the correlation between customer satisfaction and growth in customer numbers over a three-year period.[12] The report concluded that of the major banks, ANZ had the highest customer satisfaction scores and the strongest customer growth numbers. To complete the loop, an examination of the total shareholder returns generated by the four major banks over the same three-year period showed ANZ again leading the way.[13] Put these three outcomes together and they draw a straight line between staff engagement scores, customer satisfaction figures and the quantum of total shareholder returns.

Westpac is another institution that has invested heavily in this area. It has developed an extended performance management system that links non-financial performance drivers with financial outcomes. The system contains over one hundred lead indicators, each managed with the aim of increasing shareholder value. In a market briefing, the

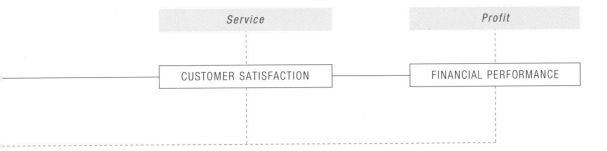

Service		Profit
CUSTOMER SATISFACTION	—	FINANCIAL PERFORMANCE

now retired CEO of Westpac, David Morgan, revealed that improving performance in just one area — employee turnover — had enabled the bank to avoid costs of $50 million per annum.[14] If Westpac can sustain this improvement over a five-year period, its shareholders are looking at an additional quarter of a billion dollars hitting the bottom line.

A Word of Caution

While the correlation between engagement and performance appears strong, a number of companies continue to generate impressive financial results even though they have alarmingly low levels of staff engagement.

For instance, Qantas has engagement scores that are reportedly, in some areas of its operations, among the lowest ever recorded in this region.[15] Interestingly, this poor performance has not prevented management from operating what is widely regarded as one of the most successful and profitable airlines in the world. How can this be?

To explain this and other anomalies, we need to look at the market in which a business operates. In open markets, with low barriers to entry, where customers can easily switch between providers, employee engagement is an excellent indicator of performance. Conversely, in closed markets where there is a monopoly or duopoly in operation and where customer choice is limited, the connection between engagement and performance is more tenuous. Under these market conditions, organisations with low staff engagement scores can still deliver impressive results.

To be fair, many leadership teams have sniffed the wind of change.

The issue is, for how much longer can they generate these results? At what point will the combination of increased marketplace competition and a shrinking labour pool force them to reconsider their approach? To be fair, many leadership teams — including Qantas', who have put in place a five-year plan to turn around staff attitudes — have sniffed the wind of change and are actively taking steps to lift their workforce's engagement levels.

This chapter contains just a few examples from the growing body of evidence that links high staff engagement scores with superior financial performance. Executives wanting to improve their company's performance would benefit greatly from using this evidence to develop a clear and compelling business case for setting up an employee engagement program inside their organisation.

CHAPTER 3

Explaining Employee Engagement

What exactly is employee engagement? While many descriptions have been written, most dissolve into instantly forgettable jargon, only adding to the confusion surrounding an already complex subject. For some, engagement is about "winning hearts and minds". For others, it is "a gauge of employee involvement and enthusiasm". And there are still more who talk about engagement as "the extent to which employees are committed to their role, their team, the business and its objectives".

Though these definitions are all unquestionably correct, they are also, at least for the employee engagement novice, dangerously narrow in their frame of reference. They talk about engagement in terms of motivating employees, but conspicuously fail to mention the importance of first addressing more fundamental issues, such as the level of satisfaction employees derive from their work.

A simple and easy-to-remember explanation of employee engagement can be found in the five-letter acronym, SAUCE.

Satisfaction + Awareness + Understanding + Commitment = Engagement

This acronym presents employee engagement as an equation in which management teams need to lift satisfaction and awareness levels before they can commence the task of building employee understanding and commitment. Outlined on the following pages, is a summary of the tasks executives might carry out in each of these areas.

Satisfaction

Employee dissatisfaction is a major obstacle to building engagement levels inside an organisation. It is highly unlikely that unhappy workers will enthusiastically participate in a company-wide discussion on the crucial subjects of workplace performance and productivity. To overcome this understandable intransigence, the leadership team needs to first identify and then eliminate the sources of their employees' dissatisfaction.

A research program consisting of interviews, focus groups and surveys will help pinpoint the specific causes of dissatisfaction. This investigative work tends to uncover universal themes such as: unchallenging work, inflexible work practices, and a lack of decision-making autonomy.

Importantly, no matter how unpalatable, every employee needs to hear the findings from this research. Sharing the results with the entire workforce helps bridge the gap between *'us'* and *'them'*, and demonstrates to everyone inside the business that the leadership team is at last beginning to listen.

Once the issues are on the table, the CEO needs to make a public commitment to eradicate them. It will be impossible to sort out every problem straightaway, but acknowledging that they exist and delivering some quick, highly visible improvements will buy time until more enduring solutions can be constructed and put in place.

The key aim of the awareness stage is to help everyone grasp why change isn't an option, but an imperative.

Awareness

As soon as employees are convinced that the leadership team is genuinely concerned about their welfare, the organisation can move onto the next step in the engagement process. This is where the team sets out to raise awareness of the issues confronting the business, so they can set the vision and strategy in context.

To do this effectively the leadership team needs to present an issue that creates an internal sense of urgency and spurs the workforce into action.

A crisis, such as a dramatic profit fall, makes this a straightforward assignment. The trick here is to present the danger in such a way that the workforce doesn't become paralysed with fear. The CEO needs to highlight the threat, while reassuring everyone that the leadership team has a plan in hand to deal with it.

More often though, there is no immediate threat on the horizon. In this situation, the leadership team needs to rally employees around the exciting opportunities that lie ahead. The communication challenge is to persuade employees that any proposed changes are in their interests as well as those of the business.

The key aim of the awareness stage is to help everyone grasp why change isn't an option, but an imperative. Only then, will employees feel compelled to dismantle old orthodoxies and adopt new ways of working.

While building intellectual understanding is difficult, it is a breeze compared to the task of generating emotional commitment.

Understanding

Once the leadership team has the workforce's undivided attention, it can open a company-wide conversation on the topics of ideology and strategy. Employees need to be clear about two things: where they are going and how they can get there.

Management needs to invest substantial resources — time and money — into communicating this important information to employees. Disseminating a clear mission and establishing a shared way of thinking and operating is the only way to move everyone in the business onto the same page.

Firms that generate a high level of internal alignment will, in effect, have provided every member of staff with their very own Global Positioning System. Hard-wired into their brain, this navigational tool will enable individuals to work out corporate longitude and latitude and consequently the next step they should take in just about any given situation at work. This is a critical part of the engagement equation, as employees need to see and understand the big picture before they can take their place in it.

Commitment

While building intellectual understanding is difficult, it is a breeze compared to the task of generating emotional commitment. Leadership teams that want to lift their organisation's engagement levels need to win their employees' hearts. For companies operating with large numbers of disengaged workers, this is an arduous undertaking.

Turning people from *'victims'* into *'volunteers'* is a long-term project. Unfortunately there are few, if any, shortcuts. If executives want to create a culture that inspires and motivates, they need to take the time to eradicate the toxic emotions that are draining energy and enthusiasm from the workplace.

The good news is, once employees can see things are changing, they'll begin to adjust their attitudes and behaviours. If they feel trusted and valued, they'll gradually turn into *'volunteers'*; willing participants who are prepared to exert the discretionary effort that is necessary to ensure that what needs to be done, gets done.

Engagement

Using the SAUCE acronym — Satisfaction + Awareness + Understanding + Commitment = Engagement: can help leadership teams to quickly grasp the basic principles that underpin the engagement process. Beware though; the simplicity of this acronym can imply that the task of generating engagement is relatively undemanding. The reality is very different. It is an extremely challenging assignment as everything that happens to an employee while they are at work — no matter how trivial — has the potential to either develop or destroy their sense of engagement. The test for the team is to manage this detail so the business can drive up its engagement scores.

CHAPTER 4

Getting to the Heart of Employee Engagement

Let's look for a moment at the term *'employee engagement'*, and consider why the person who first coined the phrase, selected the precise word, *'engagement'*.

At first glance, the word can appear dry, mechanistic even. Probe a little deeper and it becomes apparent the use of the word is meant to convey the very opposite of mechanistic. In fact, when used correctly, the word *'engagement'* connotes associations of harmony, cordiality and unity, and organisations should use these terms to guide the development of their engagement plans.

If you find this too *'soft and fluffy'*, take a moment to look up the word *'engagement'* in a dictionary. The first definition you'll come across is the one that refers to the age-old ritual of young men going down on bended knee to ask for their loved one's hand in marriage. If we reflect on how these loving relationships generally develop and evolve over time, this definition becomes particularly illuminating.

This is how it tends to go. At the outset of their life together the newly betrothed are blissfully happy. They share the same hopes and dreams, they communicate easily and frequently with one another and there is a high level of mutual trust and respect. Then they tie the knot and in a large number of cases, things begin to go downhill. Marriage guidance counsellors hear the same old stories: "we don't talk anymore", "he takes me for granted", "all she does is criticise me". The end result is, typically, a bitter parting.

Substitute a marriage contract for an employment contract and you'd probably be able to recount almost the same story. Initial excitement and enthusiasm gradually

To extend the marriage analogy, managers and workers end up like couples who no longer converse across the breakfast table.

waning as the employer-employee relationship disintegrates into thinly disguised hostility and resentment. This breakdown in workplace relations occurs because of an absence of trust between leaders, managers and team members. If these groups distrust each other, then acrimony will almost certainly become a permanent fixture inside the workplace. This in turn breeds a culture in which leaders and managers blame and berate the people they work with; which inevitably leads to problems.

Foremost among these problems will be the large number of employees who subconsciously decide to withdraw their emotional involvement and commitment from the workplace. They don't want these acrimonious exchanges to affect them, so they emotionally disengage. To extend the marriage analogy, managers and workers end up like couples who no longer converse across the breakfast table. The problem is no longer one of anger, but of apathy.

It is imperative that the leadership team finds a remedy to this situation. While part of the solution involves dismantling the internal systems and structures that underpin the problem, the bigger part lies in addressing the difficult issue of how individuals at every level in the workforce deal with and relate to one another.

The leadership team needs to deploy a personal development program that helps everyone to become more aware of the impact they have on the people around them. The core of this work involves assisting employees — especially senior leaders and managers — to more effectively manage and control their behaviour.

For this reason, leadership teams need to target most of their resources at middle management.

Once again we can learn from the example of the ANZ. Its *Breakout* program has played a major role in transforming the culture and performance of the business. The program includes a mix of sessions covering issues such as emotional intelligence, trust and communication that help employees to undergo their own transformation. On first reading, the aim of this program can sound almost Machiavellian, but it's not: employees' satisfaction and engagement levels have soared since the program was first introduced over seven years ago. *(Read the ANZ case study in Chapter 8 for more details on this remarkable program).*

Running this type of initiative is the first step in helping employees to develop more harmonious and productive relationships with their colleagues. For many, this will be the first time they've thought about what drives them, what makes them behave the way they do, and what they can do to better manage their behaviour.

Most of the workforce will enjoy this process of self-examination, enthralled to discover they are free to choose their attitude and approach. However, some may find this process more challenging.

While senior executives and team members have much to gain from adopting a more open and collaborative approach, one group may perceive that they have much to lose from the introduction of this new philosophy: middle management. Until now they have been able to retain and wield power. Now they have to embrace a whole new way of working and it can make them understandably nervous.

Previously, they were the conduits through which employees received instructions; their new position is more akin to that of captain-coach. In this new role they need to enable and support the people in their team. They need to shift their approach from controlling to coaching and, as anyone who has attempted to lose weight or give up smoking will testify, breaking well-entrenched patterns of behaviour is never easy.

For this reason, leadership teams need to target most of their resources at middle management. Thankfully, this investment will prove to be a sound one. If the leadership team can turn middle managers into engagement champions — who challenge, motivate and support the people on their team — the climate within the business will inexorably begin to improve.

As the environment starts to improve, people will consider reopening long-closed communication channels. And once senior leaders, middle managers and workers start to communicate more openly and honestly with each other, a more mature and constructive relationship can develop between all parties.

This is what happened at Vodafone's call-centre when management decided to remove the prescriptive guidelines that dictated how staff should deal with customers who had a problem or complaint. Management assumed the stance that employees know the customer best — what their problems are, and what it takes to keep them happy — so they would trust them to do the right thing without having to refer back to their manager or a rulebook. The initiative was a huge success, with positive feedback

*This additional work is fundamental
to securing the success of the
engagement program.*

from customers and staff. And interestingly, the number of call credits (refunds) issued went down as soon as the people on the frontline were in control of the system.

Of course, a turnaround in behaviour won't occur solely because of one intervention. An enormous amount of work is required to fill the vacuum created by the elimination of the chain of command. This work includes tasks such as re-engineering the organisation's structures to make them more streamlined, implementing a performance management system that helps employees align their actions with the company's goals, and reworking remuneration policies so they reward employees not only for *'what'* they do, but crucially, for *'how'* they do it.

This additional work is fundamental to securing the success of the engagement program. Without it, the *'soft stuff'*, as many managers call this type of behavioural work, will stand little or no chance of succeeding.

CHAPTER 5

Linking Employee Engagement to Results

Executives who succumb to the alluring belief that creating a *'happy'* workforce will improve their organisation's financial performance are making a mistake. Investing large sums of money into an employee wellbeing program may lift staff satisfaction levels, but that doesn't necessarily mean there will be a corresponding shift in the numbers that appear in the profit and loss statement.

This raises an issue that sits at the heart of all human capital development work: should executives plan and operate their program for the benefit of employees or the business? The answer to this question is simple: senior executives should design and run their program so it delivers clear benefits to both parties — employees *and* the business. However, for the program to be a quantifiable and sustainable success, these executives need to make the raising of revenue and profit lines their ultimate goal.

It is these two figures, revenue and profit, that tell the financial markets whether a business is winning or losing. Other measures may indicate that an organisation is heading in the right direction, but the majority of fund managers and retail shareholders base their investment decisions on hard, not soft numbers.

Conveniently, creating a link between employee performance and profit has never been easier. It's a comparatively simple task to connect the organisation's vision to the strategy, the strategy to the objectives, the objectives to the priorities, the priorities to departmental goals, and so on down the line, until everyone can see the link between their work and the bottom line.

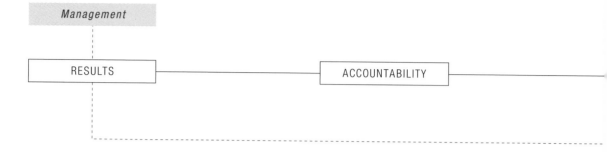

This cascading of responsibility through an organisation's chain of command is appealing, as it seemingly pushes accountability for results and performance deep into the bowels of the business. But the efficacy of this approach is an illusion. The truth of the matter is, management can't make their employees accountable for results by decree. Employees need to feel personally responsible for their work before they'll begin to accept accountability for it.

Cracking the *'personal responsibility'* code entails moving workers from a mindset of denial and excuses, to a mindset that says, "If this goes wrong, it's down to me." Executives who are asking their people to make this transition need to understand the size of the task that lies ahead of them.

The challenge boils down to a simple issue: the majority of employees have been programmed to avoid taking responsibility for their work. Experience has taught them that there can be a high price associated with sticking your hand up and saying, "I'll take care of that." Inside the wrong business, with the wrong culture, this simple act of taking ownership provides underhanded managers and colleagues with the opportunity to shift the blame when things go wrong.

Workers only need to witness or experience this amoral act once or twice before they decide that the wisest course of action is to sit on their hands. A leadership team that has a workforce operating with this mindset will face substantial performance problems — faltering quality, declining service levels, plummeting productivity.

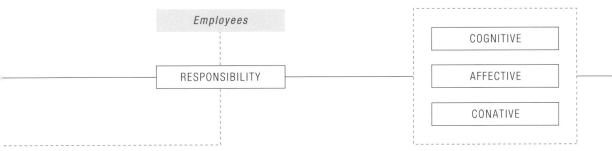

When senior executives become understandably angry about these problems and the lack of accountability demonstrated by their people, it only entrenches the attitudes that created this mindset in the first place.

To rectify this problem, the leadership team needs to diagnose its underlying cause. What is making employees behave in this manner? What is stopping them from taking ownership of their work? In nearly every instance, it's a culture-driven problem in which the organisation's culture has taught people to avoid taking responsibility. To undo this learnt behaviour the leadership team needs to transform their employees' attitudes and behaviours, to change what it is that they're thinking, feeling and doing.

It is this trio — head, heart and hands — that are at the centre of every successful engagement program. If senior executives can bring these three aspects into alignment, employees will steadily move from disengaged to engaged.

Handled correctly, this work delivers a mix of cognitive, affective and conative interventions that help employees to perform at their peak. Outlined in the following paragraphs is a summary of the work executives might carry out in each of these areas.

Cognitive interventions convey to employees what it is they need to know if they are to do their work as effectively as possible. Strategy workshops, business literacy programs and team huddles can all provide employees with a coherent perspective on what is going on inside and outside the business. This ongoing education program helps them grasp exactly what it is they need to do if the organisation is to achieve its objectives. Gradually, because everyone is heading in the same direction for the same reason, workforce alignment becomes a reality instead of an unattainable dream.

Affective interventions help employees to connect with their emotions and thought patterns. Until people understand the seeds of their behaviour they can struggle to rid themselves of toxic emotions like anger, anxiety and apathy. Personal development courses and values programs help mark out the boundaries of acceptable behaviour within the organisation. It needs to be made clear that individuals who refuse to operate within these boundaries will need to find employment elsewhere. This is harsh, but entirely necessary if a climate of openness, honesty and trust is to take root.

Conative interventions help employees shift from thinking mode to doing mode. It is easy to overlook the fact that changing some aspect of employee behaviour is a core objective of every engagement program. Consider for example a team meeting that is focused on improving productivity levels. In this meeting, is the team leader explicit about what the team should start doing differently? And more importantly, as they walk out of the door, is each worker clear about the individual changes they need to make? The leadership team has to put in place communication and remuneration policies that enable and encourage employees to take ownership of their work.

The desired outcome from this activity is for each and every employee to understand the importance of their role, to feel personally responsible for their actions, and most importantly, to feel accountable for the results they deliver.

CHAPTER 6

Measuring Employee Engagement

In order to effectively link employee engagement to results, a leadership team needs to firstly quantify the current engagement level of its workforce. Many of those who are new to the subject of employee engagement feel ill prepared for this task. To them, the whole process of conducting a survey appears to be a minefield. "Do we really need to conduct a survey?" "How do we run a survey?" "What do we do with the results?"

To answer these and other questions, I asked Hamish Deery, Regional Executive Director at Towers Perrin-ISR — one of the world's leading research organisations in this area — to share his thoughts on what it takes to run a successful engagement survey.

The first question is a simple one: "Do organisations need to measure their employees' engagement levels?" His response is unequivocal: "If organisations aren't measuring engagement they don't know where to focus their efforts. What we often find is that the drivers of engagement vary from company to company and from operating unit to operating unit. So if you're not measuring engagement and the things that drive it, you can be left focusing your interventions in the wrong areas."

Deery makes an important point: a well-designed survey generates much more than a single quantitative measure of workforce engagement. The results from the survey can provide management with a clear picture of the *'people'* problems and opportunities that exist inside their business, which in turn presents them with a precise plan of attack.

The next question put to Deery is whether companies should run their own survey. "Honestly, I think it's hard for an organisation to run its own engagement survey without having benchmarks and without staff worrying about confidentiality," he says. The confidentiality issue is understandable, but why the need for benchmarks? Why does a company need to compare its performance in this area with other companies?

Deery explains his reasoning. "If you ask people, 'Is your pay equitable to the market?' it's likely you'll get a favourable response rate of 30 to 40 per cent. Without a benchmark you might look at that answer and say, 'Gee, we've got a real issue with our pay and benefits', yet the reality is that every company in Australia struggles to get a score above 40 per cent on a pay and benefits question. So if you conduct your own survey you run the risk of focusing on low scoring issues that aren't really issues at all."

Another potential hazard lies in wait on the internet. Numerous research firms, consultancies and industry bodies have published lists that identify *'The Top 10 Drivers of Employee Engagement'*. A typical list looks something like this:

#01   Senior leadership behaviour
#02   Relationship with immediate manager
#03   Interesting and challenging work
#04   Opportunities to grow and develop
#05   Involvement in decision-making
#06   Authority to exercise discretion
#07   A collaborative corporate culture

"…every company in Australia struggles to get a score above 40 per cent on a pay and benefits question."

#08   Effective internal communications

#09   Appropriate tools and training

#10   Supportive systems and structures

On viewing these lists, some executives decide to bypass the measurement stage and instead use the information contained on these lists to develop their engagement strategy. This approach seemingly offers many advantages. It circumvents the need to conduct a survey, thus neatly sidestepping a substantial expense. Bypassing the survey also saves time, enabling the leadership team to commence its remedial work without delay. And because the lists are typically the aggregate of a large number of survey responses from different countries, cultures and companies, they present a broadly accurate picture of what drives engagement.

However, Deery voices a note of caution. "I believe that you can't use a cookie cutter approach to drive engagement. While a list from an internet site can give you a starting point, again the risk is, you'll end up focusing on issues that aren't really issues. The important thing with driving engagement is to take very focused actions in areas that you know are going to give you the biggest return on investment. Running a survey with benchmarks allows you to do that with confidence."

If the expert's advice is for companies to avoid running their own survey or building their people strategy around a list of engagement drivers sourced from the web, what

The situation inside professional services firms demonstrates why this preparatory work is essential.

can they do instead? One option is to work with an independent quantitative research specialist. But, by what criteria should a business select its research partner?

Price, expertise, experience and personal chemistry all have a part to play in the selection process. In addition, Deery suggests companies should look at the philosophical differences between suppliers.

"Some firms take a very simple view of the world," says Deery. "They have an approach that says our model will work in any environment, any industry, any business. The beauty of a simple model is it's simple. When the business gets its score back it has fewer issues to focus on, but what it won't necessarily know is what's driving the result.

"There are other firms that say the world is not that simple. They offer a customised approach that takes into account a client's unique business, context and strategy. The survey result helps management to understand where they are performing well, where the gaps are, and where, given limited resources, they should focus their efforts.

"It gets back to the question of: 'what does the business need this tool to do?' Some executives say, 'I want something that is contained from a measurement perspective, something that is very focused,' whereas others say, 'We understand our business is complex and we want to make sure we capture that complexity in our survey'."

Taking note of Deery's suggestion will facilitate the decision-making process — carefully define your company's circumstances and needs, then select the firm that best meets those needs.

When you have a research partner on board, it's time to commence the survey process. Deery is happy to throw some light on the process by sharing his firm's three-phased approach, which he labels *'ask, analyse, act'*. However, he is also keen to point out that each research firm has a bespoke methodology that no doubt confers its own unique advantages.

"Our first phase, *'ask'*, focuses on the preparations for the survey," says Deery. "We interview executives, asking them lots of questions: 'What's your business strategy?', 'What's your HR strategy?', 'What do you identify as your major people issues?', 'What do you want to get out of this process?' and 'What will success look like?'."

Deery says this work shapes the content of the survey. "We map the presenting issues against the content of the survey and that's where the customisation comes in. For example, we set up demographic questions so that during the analysis stage we can cut the data to establish whether Generation X feels differently than Generation Y on a particular issue."

The situation inside professional services firms demonstrates why this preparatory work is essential. Younger workers in these firms tend to have very different expectations of their employer than older colleagues. For example, younger workers are looking for a different offering around work-life balance and the type of culture they want to work in. Many professional services firms are now using their survey to identify the drivers of attraction, engagement and retention for discrete groups of employees.

As an aside, Deery also mentions how his firm often works in tandem with its clients to build an end-to-end communication program around the survey. "We recommend that everything connected to the survey carries a brand, a logo. So whether we're talking about the survey, going back with the results or launching an intervention, you'll always see the same logo. This is necessary because employees can struggle to see the link between each of these events unless we make it explicit for them."

"The second phase, *'analyse'*, is where the survey goes live," continues Deery. "Employees fill out their survey either online, or with paper and pencil. As they fill out the surveys we feed back the completion rates to the client literally in real time, so they can encourage their people to participate. Once the survey cuts off, we start analysing the data and generating our report."

This is an appropriate moment to explain why some research firms undertake a *'key driver analysis'* of the survey data. A brain numbing explanation runs along these lines. A *'key driver analysis'* is a post-survey study of a firm's research data that uses linear regression analysis techniques to measure the correlation between individual issues — such as leadership or culture — and employee engagement. Issues that demonstrate a high correlation are the most potent drivers of employee engagement.

Thankfully, Deery has a far simpler explanation. "Engagement is a result of doing other things well. You can't walk into a work team and say, 'you're going to be more loyal' or 'you're going to provide greater discretionary effort'. These things happen because

"...our advice is to run the survey only as often as you can act on the results and make that action visible."

people are well led, they're inspired or they feel they have empowerment in their roles. So if engagement is an outcome of many things, the *'key driver analysis'* establishes which of these has the most impact on engagement. Basically, all we are doing is using the survey data to create a roadmap of where our clients should focus their efforts."

The third and last phase, *'act'*, typically begins with a presentation to senior executives. Deery explains, "We share top line results, what's performing well and what's not performing so well against benchmark, what are the major drivers of engagement and what are the two or three things management needs to focus on if they want to enhance employee engagement."

During this phase, Deery's firm continues to talk with the leadership team about exactly who is going to lead the change and intervention process. "We clarify roles and responsibilities and, where necessary, assist the team with tasks such as results interpretation, preparing tool kits, action planning and developing interventions."

With the results delivered and action plans set in motion, the simple three-phase methodology is complete. The only remaining question is when the business should conduct its next survey. Deery has some interesting thoughts on this issue. "There is an increasing appetite for this type of information. Executives get monthly or quarterly financial reports, so they're starting to look for this type of information more regularly as well. Most companies run their survey annually, but our advice is to run the survey only as often as you can act on the results and make that action visible."

"The managing director of that business wanted to map the journey he was taking the organisation on..."

In conclusion, Deery talks about the size of the companies that Towers Perrin-ISR typically works with in this area. "The smallest company that we have worked with in the past had 80 staff, though they now employ about 500. The managing director of that business wanted to map the journey he was taking the organisation on, to put some stakes in the ground so he could assess progress along the way. Having said that, the majority of our clients would have more than 1,000 staff."

Deery says the leaders of companies with fewer than 100 employees can still get their arms around their business. They can still communicate easily with staff, know intuitively what is driving employee engagement, and get instant feedback on problems and opportunities.

While this is essentially true, many of these leaders are unsure about the strategies and tactics they should adopt if they are to lift their workforce's engagement levels. The next section of the book will provide these individuals with some useful pointers as well as providing the more experienced campaigners with a refresher on the basic concepts that underpin and drive engagement.

Employee engagement is a complex subject. It's not a single assignment; it's an intricate combination of tasks, all of which require the leadership team's full attention. What the team needs is a roadmap they can use to pull their plans into an integrated whole.

The Roadmap

On the opposite page is a list of subjects that normally find their way onto a leadership team's agenda when they first set out to lift their employees' engagement levels. Without the benefit of a quantitative research study to guide their decision-making, senior executives can find this extensive list confusing. Should they start their work in this area by addressing leadership behaviour, communicating their vision and strategy or re-engineering their internal frameworks?

What makes the situation even more perplexing is the fact that organisations are complex and unpredictable adaptive systems. Do one thing in isolation and it will almost certainly have an unimagined consequence elsewhere inside the business.

To deal with this complexity, executives need a handy roadmap that will guide and direct their efforts over, what is characteristically, an extremely long journey. This section of the book provides such a guide; an easy-to-understand chart that covers the major stopping off points. There are six stages, each linking to the next, creating a simplified overview of a typical engagement journey.

Stage 01: Appoint the engagement team and formulate a plan
Stage 02: Link strategy and execution, employees and customers
Stage 03: Align culture and brand to deliver a consistent experience
Stage 04: Prepare the foundations for the engagement program
Stage 05: Work with the four main employee engagement levers
Stage 06: Feedback the results and refresh the engagement strategy

This roadmap does not aim to deliver a definitive *'How To'* guide; the subject matter is too arcane for that. Rather, the purpose of the map is to present readers with a broad outline of the territory they are about to cover on their travels.

As with all maps, it is entirely up to the individual to select the precise route they want to follow. However, the directions, signposts and milestones presented in this section should help those who are new to this area to navigate their way.

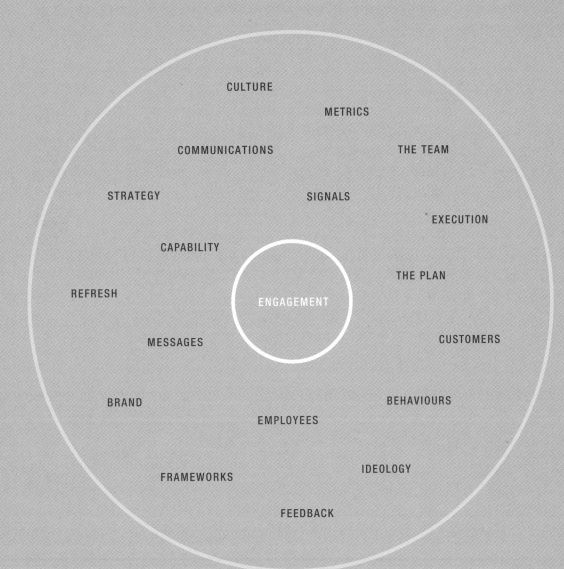

The first stage of a typical engagement journey is reassuringly straightforward. It involves the CEO appointing an engagement team and challenging this team to develop a cohesive strategy that links employee engagement to the bottom line.

Stage 01//00

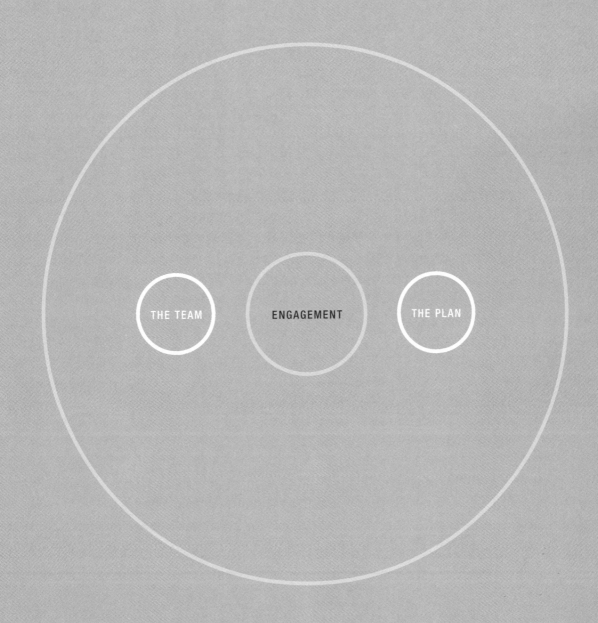

THE TEAM

ENGAGEMENT

THE PLAN

Before an engagement program can start, the CEO needs to decide who's going to run it. It is unlikely that a single person or department, no matter how talented or experienced, has the broad set of skills required to manage a comprehensive engagement program. In addition, vesting responsibility for the success of the program into a single person or department invariably leaves the rest of the business feeling absolved of responsibility if the expected improvements are a little slow to reveal themselves.

Instead of placing accountability into one area, the CEO should stretch responsibility for the success or failure of the program across the organisation. To do this, the CEO needs to appoint a cross-functional engagement team. The Head of Human Resources or the Head of Organisational Development can lead the team, but the group collectively assumes responsibility for ensuring the program achieves its stated goals and objectives.

It is crucial that the senior members of this new team carry substantial influence and power. If the team lacks authority, the workforce will assume the engagement program is a topic that they can afford to ignore. In addition, it is helpful if the team's members have strong social networks inside the business. The strength of these informal networks can help the team to push the program through any early obstacles it encounters.

The team's leader also needs to ensure this new team isn't staffed by people who are already struggling to cope with a heavy workload. If possible, some team members should be full-time appointees. This will enable these individuals to devote their entire working day to planning, implementing and evaluating major interventions. If this doesn't happen, the most disengaged people in the business will be the overworked ones on the engagement team.

Finally, there are a small, but growing number of CEOs who have decided to make the engagement team a permanent fixture inside their organisation. These CEOs create a department, most commonly titled *'People and Culture'* and staff it with individuals who either possess the skills required to run the program or know where to source those skills externally. Although this could merely be a reflection of the CEOs' commitment to the task, companies that go down this path tend to generate superior engagement scores.

ENGAGEMENT
TEAM

1

HUMAN RESOURCES   OPERATIONS

MARKETING   FINANCE

2

PEOPLE AND
CULTURE
DEPARTMENT

ACTION POINTS

#01: Appoint senior team members who carry substantial influence and power
#02: Ensure team members have strong social networks inside the business
#03: Consider creating a *'People and Culture'* department

Prior to embarking on an expedition to lift staff engagement levels, the engagement team needs to communicate to the leadership group the mechanics of their program and the precise way in which it will help the business achieve its objectives.

Without a clear understanding of how employee engagement is going to build the bottom line there is every chance senior executives will commit to the program while still having wildly different expectations of what is going to happen next.

As they discuss the program with people inside and outside the business, the subtle nuances of misinterpretation could gradually come to light. For example: At a meeting, "We're launching an engagement program; we're hoping it will stop people leaving the business." At a conference, "We're running an engagement program; we're expecting it to improve our customer service performance." And during a discussion with a journalist, "We're in the middle of an engagement program; we're anticipating it will dramatically lift our revenue and profit numbers."

The subtle differences between each of these conversations highlight how important it is to establish a shared understanding of what is going to happen once the program commences, and precisely what outcomes the business is hoping to achieve.

To create this alignment the architects of the plan need to develop a cohesive engagement strategy that communicates to the leadership team exactly how the program intends to accomplish its goals. To do this, the plan needs to explain the links between employee engagement, customer satisfaction and financial performance.

As soon as the engagement strategy document is finalised, every decision maker inside the business needs to view it and sign off on it. It is imperative the document expresses the project's objectives in numerical terms, and that the milestones towards each of these objectives are clearly marked out.

This isn't the time for hollow statements, or poorly thought out initiatives. This is where the rubber hits the road. The leadership team is more likely to deliver funding and support for the program if they can see that the business, people and engagement strategies all align and connect to the bottom line.

ENGAGEMENT STRATEGY

EMPLOYEE SATISFACTION	EMPLOYEE COMMITMENT	EMPLOYEE RETENTION
CUSTOMER SATISFACTION	CUSTOMER LOYALTY	CUSTOMER ADVOCACY
↓ COSTS	↑ REVENUE	↑ MARGINS

FINANCIAL PERFORMANCE

ACTION POINTS

#01: Develop a cohesive engagement strategy
#02: Identify the links between engagement and financial performance
#03: Ensure the program's objectives are specific and quantifiable

Once the engagement team has been appointed and an approved plan put in place, the engagement program can commence. The work in this stage revolves around an important nexus between employees, strategy, execution and customers. Executives can use their engagement program to lift performance in each of these areas.

Stage 02//00

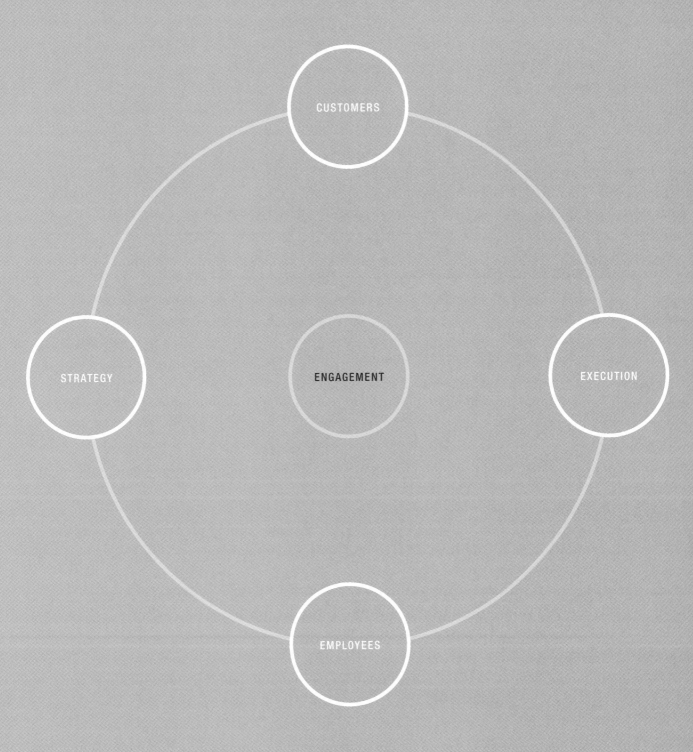

Given the undeniable importance of employees to every organisation, it makes sense for the engagement team to spend time looking at what makes them tick — what are their needs and aspirations, their fears and anxieties? This is an easier task than many executives imagine. The reason? Our drives and desires are largely universal.

We all need to earn enough money to feed and house ourselves. We all want to feel safe, both physically and psychologically. We all need to feel we are a part of a tribe; that we belong. We all yearn for recognition, to receive applause and acclaim for a job well done. And finally, we all want to realise our potential, to achieve and self-actualise.

This list, as many readers will have recognised, is Maslow's Theory of Human Motivation applied to the workplace.[16] Executives who are endeavouring to lift their workforce's engagement levels need to understand how this hierarchy of needs shapes the attitudes and behaviours of their people.

Far too many executives ignore this advice and fixate instead on their employees' lower order needs, misguidedly believing salary increases will secure their loyalty and commitment. Used in isolation, this approach no longer works.

A growing number of employees are now looking beyond the size of their pay packet to determine how much effort they'll expend at work. They are now reflecting on what their employer is doing to satisfy their higher order needs. If the answer is, "not much", these *'head-in-the-sand'* employers will end up facing one of two scenarios.

One, their employees will leave, forcing the business to incur the expense of recruiting and training replacements. Or two, their employees will hang around, but put little or no effort into their work.

To prevent this happening, executives need to tackle the source of this problem: their employees' unmet needs. The engagement team needs to identify these needs and set about satisfying them straightaway. If they don't, the organisation's engagement scores will remain stubbornly low, as employees brood over their unfulfilled hungers and desires. It's a simple *'give and get'* equation; if businesses give their people what they need, it's more likely they'll get what they want — loyalty and commitment — in return.

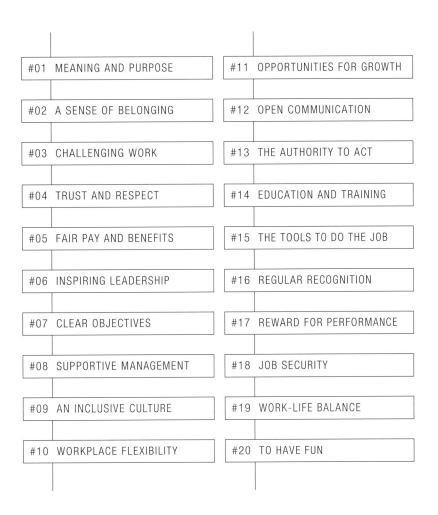

#01 MEANING AND PURPOSE	#11 OPPORTUNITIES FOR GROWTH
#02 A SENSE OF BELONGING	#12 OPEN COMMUNICATION
#03 CHALLENGING WORK	#13 THE AUTHORITY TO ACT
#04 TRUST AND RESPECT	#14 EDUCATION AND TRAINING
#05 FAIR PAY AND BENEFITS	#15 THE TOOLS TO DO THE JOB
#06 INSPIRING LEADERSHIP	#16 REGULAR RECOGNITION
#07 CLEAR OBJECTIVES	#17 REWARD FOR PERFORMANCE
#08 SUPPORTIVE MANAGEMENT	#18 JOB SECURITY
#09 AN INCLUSIVE CULTURE	#19 WORK-LIFE BALANCE
#10 WORKPLACE FLEXIBILITY	#20 TO HAVE FUN

ACTION POINTS

#01: Determine what's going on inside the hearts and minds of employees
#02: Use qualitative and quantitative research to identify employees' unmet needs
#03: Focus on employees' higher order needs: belonging, recognition and achievement

Typically, executives who are responsible for developing next year's corporate strategy go to an off-site retreat to devise their plans. Upon their return, they spend weeks fine-tuning the details, making sure they've got all their bases covered. Then, with little or no forethought they push their strategy out into the business and naively assume their colleagues will understand it. It's an ineffectual approach. If it has taken months for the smartest people in the business to create the strategy, it's totally unrealistic to expect people further down the line to comprehend it in a fraction of the time.

Given the number of companies who still distribute their plans in this manner, it isn't surprising that Kaplan and Norton found that 95 per cent of employees are either unaware of, or do not understand their organisation's strategy.[17] This statistic provides irrefutable evidence that a new approach to strategy dissemination is long overdue.

The missing piece of the strategy jigsaw is communication. Executives are failing to invest enough time, money and effort into sharing their plans with their people. A simple sporting analogy is instructive: if you want to beat the opposition, everybody on the team needs to study and understand the playbook, not just the captain. The lesson here is that management shouldn't keep their strategy hidden away; everyone needs to understand where the business is heading and how it intends to get there.

When first presenting their strategy to employees, executives need to make sure it comes across as a rousing call to action. Logic and reason have their place, but if the strategy is going to motivate the workforce it needs to exude energy and emotion. For this reason, the initial stage of a strategy presentation should be a compelling communication piece, delivered in person by the organisation's senior leadership team.

These executives need to arouse their employees' interest by making them laugh, making them gasp, doing whatever they have to, to capture their attention. Once they've got it, they need to hit them with the plan. "This is our destination, this is what we need to do to get there, and here are some milestones for us to check along the way." Everyone sees the big picture; everyone hears the same story. Using this approach is the first step towards engaging employees with the task of realising the corporate strategy.

IMPLEMENTATION

COLLABORATE	#01
FORMULATE	#02
COMMUNICATE	#03
ACTIVATE	#04
EVALUATE	#05

COMMUNICATION

#01	KICK-OFF EVENTS
#02	STRATEGY BOOKS
#03	BRIEFING PACKS
#04	TEAM BRIEFINGS
#05	TWO-WAY DIALOGUE

ACTION POINTS

#01: Develop and implement an effective internal communications strategy
#02: Involve employees by asking them their opinion of the plan at an early stage
#03: Align everyone around the company's mission, vision and strategy

Until recently, the blame for the strategy-execution gap rested largely with employees. "We showed them the strategy, we told them the goals, and they still didn't get it," was the prevailing attitude. In reality, the responsibility for this problem rests higher up, with the organisation's leaders. They're the ones who need to establish a meaningful connection between their people and their plans.

If employees don't have a clear *'line of sight'* between their work and the company's strategic goals, underperformance across a wide range of metrics is virtually inevitable. To deal with this problem, the engagement team needs to find a way of making the company's strategy an integral part of every employee's day.

The solution to this challenge is implementing a performance management system that opens up an organisation-wide conversation around the company's objectives, strategies and results. This is not a prescription for more top-down management; the aim is to present each person in the business with a clear view of what is happening and why, so they can get on with their work without unnecessary interference from above.

It is critical this system allows time at the start of the cycle for employees to discuss with their manager, either collectively or individually, their role in executing the plan. Some executive teams are finding that simple strategy maps can help people to have these conversations. Facilitated group discussions centred on these maps presents employees with the opportunity to question the detail of the plan, which in turn enables them to clarify their own goals and priorities.

The performance management system also needs to incorporate regular one-on-one reviews, so managers can deliver their people feedback on how they, and the rest of the business are performing. This keeps everyone focused on executing the plan, and provides managers with the opportunity to coach their people through any difficulties they are encountering.

Establishing a clear *'line of sight'* for employees drags strategy out of the boardroom and into the business. And the further the leadership team drive their plans into the business, the better the results.

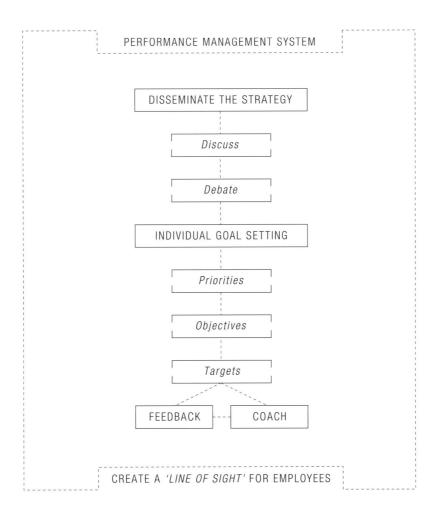

PERFORMANCE MANAGEMENT SYSTEM

DISSEMINATE THE STRATEGY

Discuss

Debate

INDIVIDUAL GOAL SETTING

Priorities

Objectives

Targets

FEEDBACK — — — COACH

CREATE A *'LINE OF SIGHT'* FOR EMPLOYEES

ACTION POINTS

#01: Ensure employees understand their role in executing the corporate strategy
#02: Implement a performance management system that puts everyone in the picture
#03: Set goals and make sure managers run feedback sessions with their people

Customer satisfaction, customer loyalty, and customer advocacy are the metrics a business needs to lift in order to turn its engagement efforts into increased revenue.

However, developing a customer-focused culture remains an elusive goal for most executives. The reason for this is that many management teams adopt a prescriptive and inflexible approach with their employees when it comes to formulating their customer service strategies. They believe that creating a customer charter and tightly policing it will enable them to achieve the results they are after, but this is seldom the case.

This rigid approach falls short on three counts. First, it makes no allowance for the importance of internal service quality. How individuals, teams, and departments interact and support each other is a key determinant of external service quality. Second, it overlooks the fact that outstanding customer service is so much more than exchanging pleasantries; frontline employees need the training, tools and authority to satisfactorily address customer enquiries and problems. And third, failing to involve employees in formulating a plan to tackle the customer service problem all but guarantees failure, as without employee involvement, there is no employee commitment.

The engagement team can circumvent these problems by helping employees to hear the voice of the customer. This should not be a generic exercise about the importance of providing good service; it needs to be specific to an organisation's people, products and clientele. Ideally, the team should map the service and take the entire workforce on a typical customer journey — showing them the customer experience from start to finish.

This helps employees to see what is working and, more importantly, what isn't. Once they see where the problems are, they're usually keen to put things right. The trick here is to avoid having consultants step in. Organisations enjoy more success when they challenge their employees to design and develop solutions to the problems they've personally witnessed. Given the opportunity and the right support, the people who work inside the system will come up with more effective remedies than external experts. The benefit of using this approach is that employees will own the solution and as a result, will do everything in their power to make sure it works.

EMPLOYEE INVOLVEMENT AND COMMITMENT

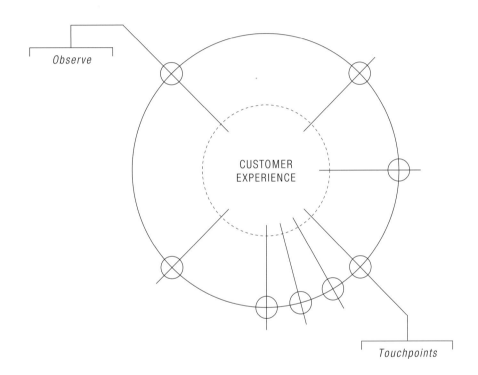

Observe

CUSTOMER
EXPERIENCE

Touchpoints

CUSTOMER SATISFACTION, LOYALTY AND ADVOCACY

ACTION POINTS

#01: Focus on and measure internal service quality: it influences external service quality
#02: Re-engineer internal systems and structures to facilitate service delivery
#03: Ask employees to develop solutions: it secures their involvement and commitment

FIG. N⁰ 0204

Culture and brand are two powerful forces. They influence the attitudes and behaviours of customers and employees. Engagement teams who want their plans to succeed need to bring their culture and brand into alignment, so they deliver a consistent experience to internal and external audiences.

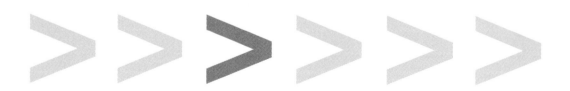

Stage 03//00

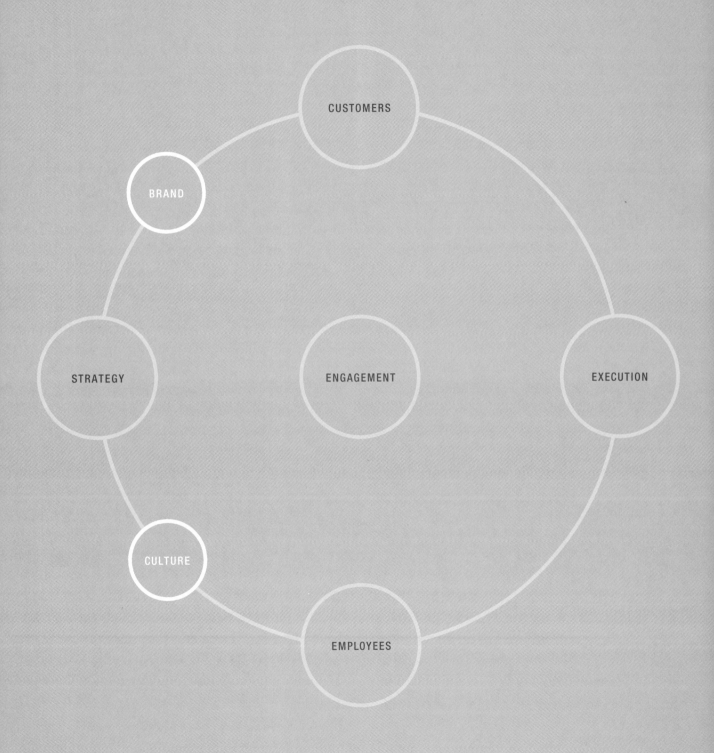

At some point, every engagement program runs into the thorny issue of culture. Some executives are tempted to bypass this stage of work, as their company's culture can appear unmanageable. However, culture is clearly revealed by the behaviours and practices exhibited throughout an organisation and the ability to observe a culture in action means it is a subject executives can analyse, measure and if necessary, change.

When first working in this area, it helps if the engagement team has a clear understanding of how an organisation's culture develops and evolves over time. It's a simple process — leadership behaviour generates values, values build beliefs, beliefs harden to become assumptions, and eventually these assumptions turn into firmly-held attitudes that aggregate to become an organisation's behavioural norms.

When an outsider witnesses these norms, they register them as a company's unique and distinctive culture. It's what makes customers say, "They were so incredibly helpful," or "I'm never going there again."

Inside a business, these behavioural norms exert an even more powerful influence. It's a force we've all experienced when starting a new job. On our first day we feel uneasy. We've no idea how anything works or how we'll fit in with our colleagues. Somehow though, by the end of the month we know exactly how the place functions and if we're smart, we'll have figured out how we need to behave if we're going to get along.

We glean this knowledge from being immersed in our new culture: we observe how decisions are made, we witness the practice of rites, rituals and routines and we listen to the stories people tell. It's a remarkably efficient method of cultural contagion. Not only does it fast track the assimilation of new recruits into the business, it continuously reinforces key aspects of the organisation's culture to existing staff.

If an engagement initiative is to succeed, management needs to actively manage their organisation's culture. Fortuitously, the engagement levers referred to later in this book are identical to those used to shape and influence culture. Executives, who plan their interventions carefully, can simultaneously re-engineer their organisation's culture at the same time as they build their staff engagement levels.

LEADERSHIP
BEHAVIOUR

VALUES

FOCUS ON
CHANGING
BEHAVIOURS

BELIEFS

EMPLOYEE
BEHAVIOUR

ASSUMPTIONS

NORMS

ATTITUDES

ACTION POINTS

#01: Start culture change at the top, with the senior leadership team

#02: Focus on changing behaviours: not beliefs, assumptions or attitudes

#03: Signal change through the establishment of new rites, rituals and routines

Many brands fail to bridge the gap between what's expected and what's experienced. To correct this oversight, organisations need to rethink the way they approach the brand development process. As it stands, most executives who are developing a brand will prepare a brief and approach an advertising agency. The very best of these agencies respond not with a creative execution, but with a brand model. At the centre of this model sits the brand promise, the snappy one-liner that communicates the brand's essence.

These models are very persuasive and they work. They guide the development of advertising that entices members of the public into spending their hard-earned money. The problems begin when these potential customers attempt to make their purchase. Is the employee who is dealing with them aware of the new campaign? Perhaps. Do they understand the brand promise? Possibly. Are they able to deliver the promise? Unlikely. Will the potential customer be disappointed? Almost certainly.

It's here, at the point of sale, that the advertising industry frequently drops the ball. They make the brand promise on their client's behalf, but then do precious little to help deliver it. Closing the gap between *'say'* and *'do'* entails making the brand on the inside the same as the one on the outside. There are two ways executives can tackle this assignment; only one of them works.

The most commonly used approach involves running a workshop that helps staff to *'live the brand'*. This is typically a half-day seminar that takes employees through an overview of the new brand promise and how they should deliver it. However, this type of event rarely delivers the hoped-for results, because it's unrealistic to expect a one-off workshop to bring about a lasting change in employee behaviour.

A more effective strategy is to go back to the beginning and build the brand around the workforce's values, beliefs and behaviours. Approaching the task in this way is far more challenging, but it is more practical and confers a significant competitive advantage. This advantage accrues because brands built around *'people and culture'* are more easily differentiated in the marketplace, and crucially, once successful, are virtually impossible for competitors to copy.

```
                          ┌──────────────┐
                          │              │
                          │    BRAND     │
      ┌─→                 │   PROMISE    │                 ┐
                          │              │                 ↓
                          └──────┊───────┘

  ┌──────────────┐              EMPLOYEES              ┌──────────────┐
  │              │            ─────────────            │              │
  │   CUSTOMER   │┊ ┊ ┊ ┊ ┊ ┊              ┊ ┊ ┊ ┊ ┊ ┊│   CUSTOMER   │
  │  EXPERIENCE  │              CUSTOMERS              │  EXPECTATION │
  │              │                                     │              │
  └──────────────┘                                     └──────────────┘

                          ┌──────────────┐
      ↑                   │              │                 ┐
      └                   │    BRAND     │                 ↵
                          │   REALITY    │
                          │              │
                          └──────────────┘
```

ACTION POINTS

#01: Build the brand around the workforce's values, beliefs and behaviours

#02: Align the internal and external brand promises

#03: Focus on developing the workforce's ability to deliver the brand promise

Before the engagement program can move into full operational mode, the team needs to lay some important foundations. Too often programs falter over the basics. The team needs to address issues such as workforce capability before they can start to efficiently operate the main engagement levers.

Stage 04//00

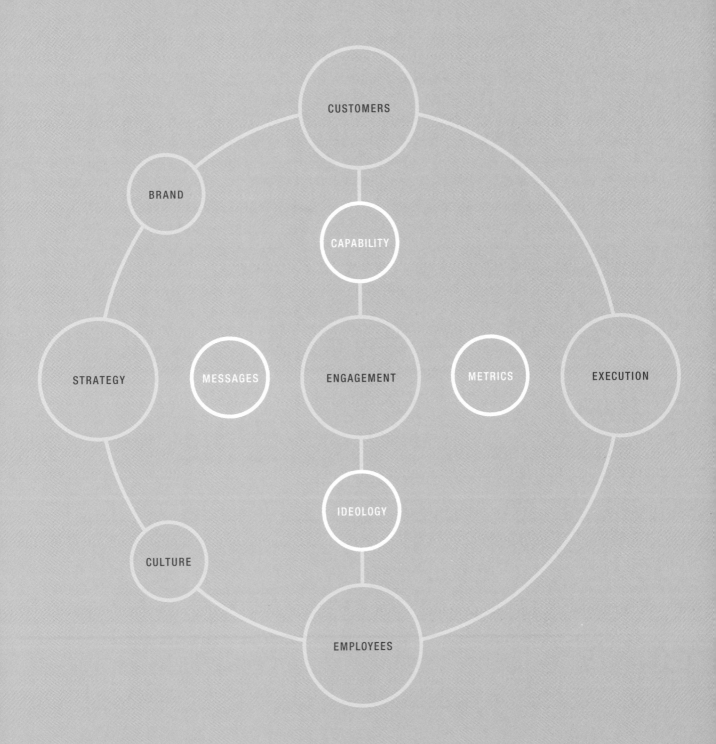

CUSTOMERS

BRAND

CAPABILITY

STRATEGY

MESSAGES

ENGAGEMENT

METRICS

EXECUTION

IDEOLOGY

CULTURE

EMPLOYEES

© INSIDE RESEARCH

It is impossible for workers to feel engaged if they don't understand the corporate strategy and lack the information they need to do their work. If the engagement team is to fix this oversight, they need to develop a message delivery system that enables employees to become more informed and involved — important precursors to their becoming engaged. This requires the team to complete three tasks.

The first task is to reduce the number of messages that are in circulation. Technology has made it too easy to push information out into a business, and consequently, many workers suffer communication overload. To alleviate this burden, executives need to find out how long it takes people to plough through the messages they are receiving, and simultaneously ascertain how much of this information is required. Once it becomes clear just how much irrelevant information is being pumped out, the team can turn their attention to culling all superfluous messages.

The second task is to give priority to those key messages that generate employee understanding and commitment. These communications should dominate the airwaves. Regrettably, many executives mistakenly focus their efforts on pushing out punitive messages relating to rules and regulations. When this happens day in and day out, employees tend to switch off. To prevent this, the team needs to distribute messages that help employees to understand where the business is heading and what they can do to help it get there.

The engagement team's final message management task is to co-ordinate the flow of messages, in much the same way as an air traffic controller manages the movement of aircraft. Communicators need to be clear about which messages are ready to depart, which messages have landed, and which messages are still up in the air. Send up too many messages and cranial confusion will reign, as conflicting messages clamour for the workforce's attention. Co-ordinating the delivery of information allows employees to focus their attention on those messages that will drive improvements in business performance.

If the engagement team can complete these three tasks, employees will have a much clearer understanding of their role in helping the business to succeed.

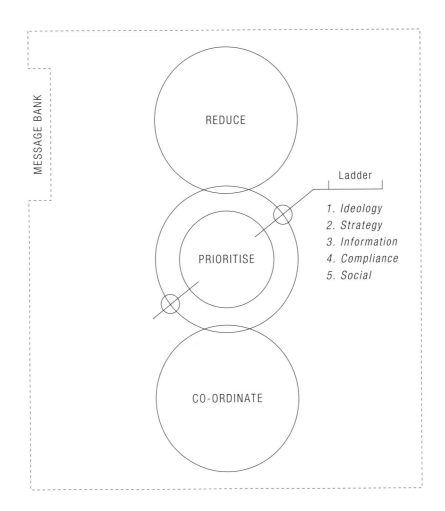

MESSAGE BANK

REDUCE

Ladder

PRIORITISE

1. *Ideology*
2. *Strategy*
3. *Information*
4. *Compliance*
5. *Social*

CO-ORDINATE

ACTION POINTS

#01: Ruthlessly reduce the number and type of messages that are in circulation

#02: Prioritise messages that generate employee understanding and commitment

#03: Co-ordinate the flow of messages so employees can focus on messages that matter

Leadership teams sometimes fail to give consideration to the question of whether their people are capable of bringing the approved corporate strategy to life. Their plans talk boldly about a new way of doing business, but neglect to address the issue of whether employees can adjust to this new way of working.

Strategy developed and executed in this way is almost certain to fail. The double-whammy is that staff engagement levels will probably nosedive at the same time.

This happens because employees who lack the resources to satisfactorily complete their work typically feel disheartened and disgruntled, neither of which are traits of the highly engaged. Conversely, employees who do possess the information, tools and training they need to do their work are usually far more committed and motivated.

To sidestep any potential problems in this area, management needs to establish their organisation's *'capability gap'*. This gap is the difference between the skills, knowledge and tools that employees currently possess and those they will require to successfully execute the new corporate strategy. The bigger the *'capability gap'*, the more remedial work the leadership team needs to do behind the scenes before they can successfully launch and execute their new corporate strategy.

Taking the time to develop a capability plan will help management to identify the training and tools employees require if they are to deliver the customer promise that underpins the new strategy. Examples of the type of programs that might need to be introduced in this area include: investing in new IT hardware and software, developing online learning facilities and providing employees with business acumen training.

Though these types of interventions do not fit within the narrowest definition of an employee engagement program, it is an area of work that often dictates whether or not the program succeeds. This is because a workforce that has to operate in an inefficient manner will always struggle to convert its efforts into bottom line dollars.

The additional benefit of this work is that it feeds directly into employees' well-known need for learning and development opportunities. It is important the engagement team exploits this link between *'personal'* and *'organisational'* development.

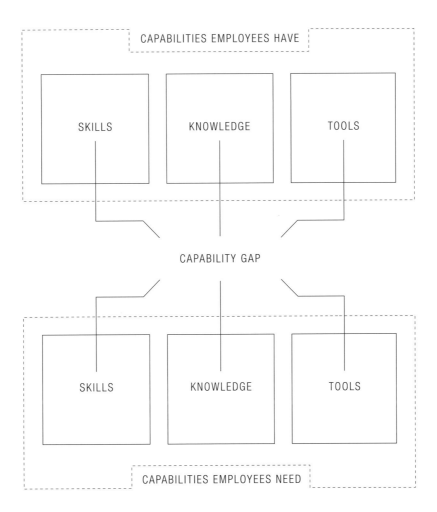

CAPABILITIES EMPLOYEES HAVE

SKILLS　　KNOWLEDGE　　TOOLS

CAPABILITY GAP

SKILLS　　KNOWLEDGE　　TOOLS

CAPABILITIES EMPLOYEES NEED

ACTION POINTS

#01: Measure the *'capability gap'*: do this before launching a new corporate strategy
#02: Develop a comprehensive capability plan to identify and remedy shortcomings
#03: Ensure employees have the skills, knowledge and tools they need to succeed

Developing and implementing a robust measurement system at the very outset of an engagement program is a crucial part of the preparation process.

Establishing the demographic profile of the workforce provides the foundations for a measurement system. What is their average age? What percentage of them are tertiary educated? What is their average length of tenure? This information will prove to be an invaluable resource by, for example, helping the team to accurately estimate future retirement rates or identify the most appropriate internal communication channels.

While ascertaining the demographic profile of the organisation is important, knowing what employees are thinking and feeling is vital. Executives need to determine the mood and mindset of their people. Are they onboard and ready to contribute? Or are they deflated and demotivated? A qualitative research study — comprised of interviews and focus groups — will provide most of the answers. The team should only progress with their engagement plans once they understand the climate inside the business.

The emergence of the employee engagement survey has helped drive people issues out of the Human Resources Department and into the executive suite. Now, managers can see with their own eyes the link between good people practices and the bottom line. What's more — and perhaps this is the reason why employee engagement has been so warmly embraced — the results of the survey reach far beyond the executive suite. Everyone gets to hear how the business is going, and, more importantly, they learn how their team or department is performing. This is powerful stuff, as everyone is asked to answer the question, "What do we need to do as a company, as a team and as individuals, to improve our performance in the areas where we are struggling?"

Beware though. There is a temptation to look at the survey score as the sole measure of success. Engagement should be a means to an end, not an end in itself. To establish if their program is bearing fruit, the team should put their engagement scores, customer satisfaction figures and profit numbers on top of their measurement dashboard. For a program to be judged a success, all three of these figures — engagement, satisfaction and profit — need to be heading in the right direction and at the right trajectory.

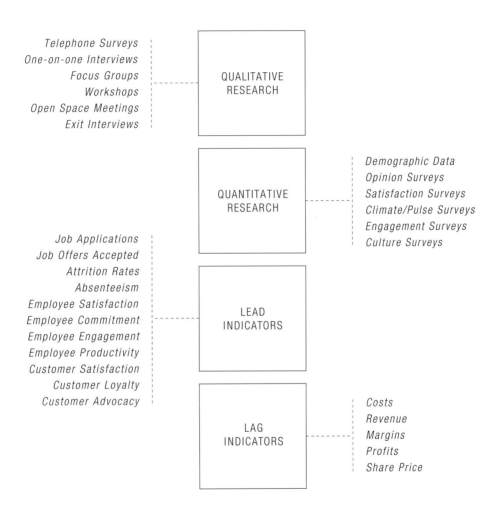

Telephone Surveys
One-on-one Interviews
Focus Groups
Workshops
Open Space Meetings
Exit Interviews

QUALITATIVE
RESEARCH

QUANTITATIVE
RESEARCH

Demographic Data
Opinion Surveys
Satisfaction Surveys
Climate/Pulse Surveys
Engagement Surveys
Culture Surveys

Job Applications
Job Offers Accepted
Attrition Rates
Absenteeism
Employee Satisfaction
Employee Commitment
Employee Engagement
Employee Productivity
Customer Satisfaction
Customer Loyalty
Customer Advocacy

LEAD
INDICATORS

LAG
INDICATORS

Costs
Revenue
Margins
Profits
Share Price

ACTION POINTS

#01: Conduct qualitative research to unearth the mood and mindset of the workforce
#02: Undertake quantitative research to obtain hard measures
#03: Link KPIs: employee engagement, customer satisfaction and financial performance

Executives who want to lift their workforce's engagement levels need to be explicit about why their business exists, where it is heading and how they want employees to behave.

If they don't do this, they are forcing their people to operate without the benefit of a clear ideology to help shape their attitudes and behaviour. This is a common mistake. Without a strong ideology to guide them, employees can flounder, unsure of what action to take unless they're receiving direct instructions from their supervisor.

To address this oversight, organisations need to align their employees around a well-defined corporate belief system. Everyone inside the business needs to understand the triumvirate of mission, vision and values — the *'Why?'* the *'Where?'* and the *'How?'*.

First, a mission statement needs to encapsulate a compelling core purpose; a reason to exist that goes beyond meeting this month's budget. This doesn't mean the bottom line isn't important. The issue is, making money for shareholders they neither know nor care about doesn't motivate most employees. They're looking for something more meaningful; they want to hear the story that will drive them to deliver the numbers.

Second, a vision needs to do more than speak of some galactically far-off future; it needs to help workers make sense of the road that lies immediately ahead. "Why are we driving costs down so aggressively?" "Why is improving customer service so important?" Articulating a short-term vision enables individuals to understand what is happening, which in turn makes it easier for them to cope with any surrounding turbulence.

And third, whether stated or unstated, an organisation's core values are continuously shaping employees' beliefs and behaviours. Identifying, clarifying and embedding values is a challenging task, but it's one every business needs to undertake. The need for this work is driven by the fact that a framework of shared values is more effective at guiding and directing behaviour than a procedures manual or rulebook.

Companies who manage to build alignment around their mission, vision and values will have hit the mother lode of employee engagement — a rich seam of motivated and committed workers who all share the same aims, ambitions and values.

BELIEF SYSTEM

PURPOSE

VISION

VALUES

WHY? —— WHERE? —— HOW?

ACTION POINTS

#01: Create a core purpose that inspires, motivates and directs behaviour
#02: Help employees to make sense of their work by communicating a clear vision
#03: Identify, clarify and embed the organisation's core values

With the foundations in place, the team can begin working with the main levers of engagement. These levers drive the biggest shifts in employee attitude and behaviour — so their judicious use is crucial.

Stage 05//00

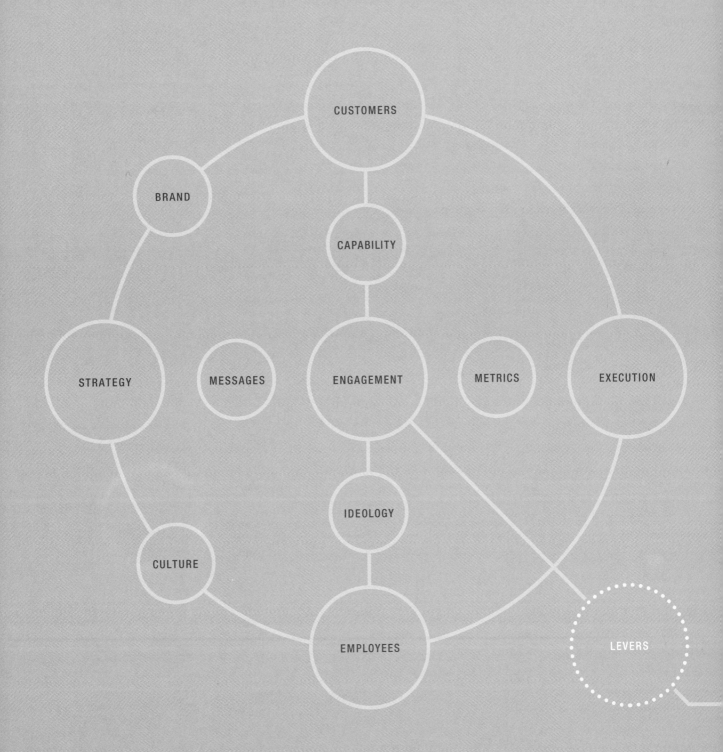

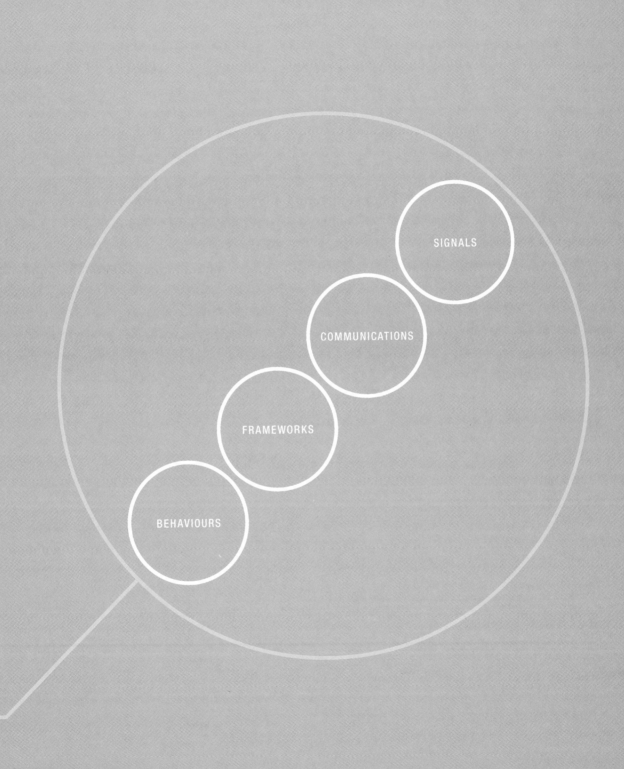

If employee engagement is about one thing more than any other, it's about the quality of relationships inside an organisation: between those at the very top and those at the very bottom, between managers and workers and, of course, between colleagues. When these relationships are strained, performance suffers. Conversely, when these relationships are harmonious, performance soars.

High-quality relationships are a by-product of people choosing to adopt positive behaviours. A leader who motivates rather than manipulates, a manager who coaches instead of controls, a colleague who collaborates rather than competes. This can sound hopelessly idealistic, but it's not as simple as nice versus nasty. It's a choice between constructive or destructive behaviour, and it's indisputable which of those delivers the best result. The problem is, many executives have forgotten how to behave constructively; their focus has been on building revenue, not relationships.

The engagement team needs to put in place a program that will help these executives to develop their *'people'* skills. This remedial work needs to commence at the top of the organisation as everyone takes their cue from the people who hold the reins of power. Only when senior executives are consistently displaying constructive behaviours will workers lower down the hierarchy deem it necessary to change their ways.

Managers need to become more aware of their behaviour, and how it affects the attitudes of the people they work with. Once they realise how damaging their actions can be — or how motivating and inspiring — they become willing to adopt and exhibit behaviours that are in keeping with those you'd expect from a more senior member of staff. The goal is to instill an overarching set of leadership behaviours that lay the foundations for a new, more open and collaborative culture.

While an education program will get things moving, it is coaching and the provision of constructive feedback that will maintain momentum. Employees who are encountering problems in adopting new behaviours need access to a coach or mentor so they can discuss alternative tactics. Similarly, receiving timely feedback on behavioural issues helps people to modify their behaviour before it becomes a career-limiting problem.

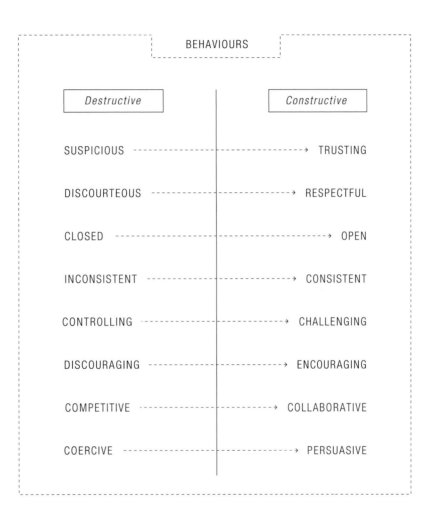

BEHAVIOURS

Destructive	*Constructive*
SUSPICIOUS	TRUSTING
DISCOURTEOUS	RESPECTFUL
CLOSED	OPEN
INCONSISTENT	CONSISTENT
CONTROLLING	CHALLENGING
DISCOURAGING	ENCOURAGING
COMPETITIVE	COLLABORATIVE
COERCIVE	PERSUASIVE

ACTION POINTS

#01: Start from the top: train leaders so they can adopt the position of captain-coach
#02: Help employees to undergo a personal transformation: destructive to constructive
#03: Utilise tools that provide leaders with quantifiable feedback on their behaviour

How an organisation manages its systems and structures will affect its staff engagement scores. Bloated bureaucracies tend to create demotivated workers with little or no sense of accountability, while misaligned processes frequently generate unforeseen and unwanted outcomes.

As a matter of urgency, senior leaders need to align their organisation's operational framework into their engagement plans. Why the rush? Employees have a propensity towards cynicism; they stop believing if they hear one thing but experience another.

Executives should start the alignment process with a review of their organisation's existing operating systems. A comprehensive audit will allow them to scrutinise key processes and practices. If these appear constipated, simplification is the best medicine. Streamlining or automating overly complex systems will allow people to work on more productive and profitable tasks.

This audit should also incorporate a review of the organisation's *'people'* policies. How a business recruits, inducts, trains, develops, coaches, appraises, recognises and rewards its people ultimately shapes their mood and mindset. If employees are to come through the door every morning revved up and ready to go, these policies need to provide them with a satisfying and rewarding work experience.

The team also needs to look at how the business is structured. They need the right people in the right roles, with the right level of accountability. To address this last point, they need to be explicit about where accountability resides. Often, it sits too low or too high. If it sits too low, employees will lack the authority to make decisions. On the other hand, if it sits too high, an entire organisation can rest on its elbows awaiting an overly long chain of command to make up its mind. Neither situation is acceptable. To resolve this problem, management needs to decide where accountability should sit and then ensure the people who carry the responsibility receive the training they need to handle it.

If possible, this work should commence before leaders announce their engagement plans to internal audiences. Executives who have been down this path before know the substance of their program is far more important than the sizzle.

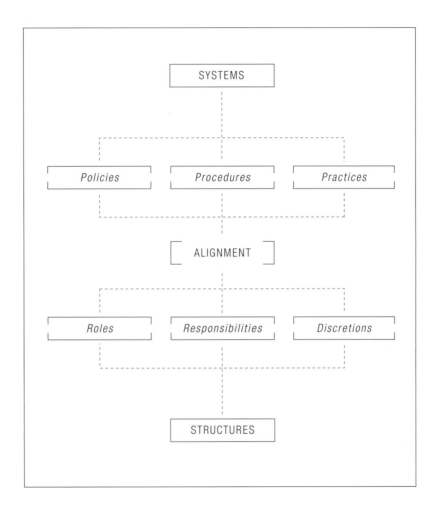

ACTION POINTS

#01: Deconstruct policies, procedures and practices and where necessary, rebuild
#02: Focus on aligning the organisation's *'people'* policies: attract, engage and retain
#03: Re-engineer internal structures: the right people in the right roles

Deploying an individual communication tool in isolation, such as a new intranet, will do little or nothing to drive engagement. Generating employee engagement requires an all-encompassing approach, one that gets everyone in the business talking to each other about the issues that matter. To achieve this goal the team needs to be adept at using all three internal communication channels — mass, group and one-to-one.

The most widely used form of communication is mass communication. This platform is used to broadcast information through media such as newsletters and emails. Working through this channel enables the team to send everyone in the business the same message at the same time. The downside is that when used on its own, this form of communication will do little or nothing to engender engagement. Employees may receive the same message, but that doesn't necessarily mean they'll understand or act on it.

To get their message across, the team needs to integrate mass communication with group communication. This involves bringing people together in small gatherings so they can absorb, question and reflect upon the communications they're receiving. These meetings give employees the opportunity to internalise the complex messages that are coming their way. The discussions help employees to collectively determine what is happening, why it is happening and most importantly, how it will affect them.

Unfortunately, many communication programs — even the good ones — stop at the group level. This is a mistake. It overlooks the fact that one-to-one communication, between manager and worker, is often the most potent form of internal communication. If an engagement program is to succeed, executives need to direct a significant proportion of their budget towards helping line managers become skilled communicators who are able to inspire, coach and connect with the people on their team. Once this channel is working effectively, engagement levels typically surge, as employees enjoy a more productive and rewarding relationship with their immediate manager.

Engagement teams should use their internal communication program to *'change the conversation'* within the organisation, so employees can begin to connect, collaborate and get things done.

COMMUNICATION CHANNELS

C1

MASS

Context

C2

GROUP

Converse

C3

ONE-TO-ONE

Coach

ACTION POINTS

#01: Ensure the communications program establishes a shared vision and agenda
#02: Give employees the chance to collectively decipher the meaning behind messages
#03: Help managers to communicate more effectively with the people on their team

---

Everything is in place and the wheels of the engagement program are beginning to turn. However progress at the outset can be painfully slow. Employees are waiting to see how committed the leadership team are to this new program. To persuade them that they're serious and that the program is here to stay, the leadership team needs to start sending out some new short- and long-term signals.

Short-term signals provide irrefutable proof that things really are going to change this time. Actions such as eliminating designated car parking spaces or closing down the executive dining room indicate that the business is going to operate in a more egalitarian manner. The workforce also wants to know where the program sits on management's agenda. Is it at the top or towards the bottom? The workforce will look to see how much time and money the leadership team is investing into the program to determine the level of importance it holds.

The leadership team also needs to lay down some long-term signals that will help guide employees as they go about their work. An organisation's values play an important role here. The values tell people what behaviour is and isn't acceptable. To reinforce this message, companies should consider establishing a recognition program that celebrates values-aligned behaviour. Lavishing the winners with praise and prizes at an awards ceremony will help shift the behaviour barometer towards a fair weather setting.

Once management has done the hard work of breaking through its workforce's existing thought patterns and beliefs, there is a risk of complacency setting in. Executives need to put in place measures that will sustain the changes they have wrought. For example, the use of storytelling techniques to establish company legend and lore is an excellent way of reminding everyone of what's important to the organisation, and why.

As work on the engagement program progresses, management needs to understand that employees will continue to look for clues as to what the future holds. Everything that happens has the potential to send them a signal. The leadership team needs to make sure that their messages are always consistent and that their actions continue to signal their commitment to the program.

SHORT-TERM SIGNALS

Indicate change is happening

Myths	*Stories*	*Legends*	*Lore*
Rituals	*Ceremonies*	*Traditions*	*Routines*
Values	*Principles*	*Beliefs*	*Ethics*
Symbols	*Gestures*	*Signs*	*Actions*

Embed change into the system

LONG-TERM SIGNALS

ACTION POINTS

#01: Start sending short- and long-term signals to signify change
#02: Use the organisation's core values to guide and direct employee behaviour
#03: Use storytelling techniques to remind people of what's important, and why

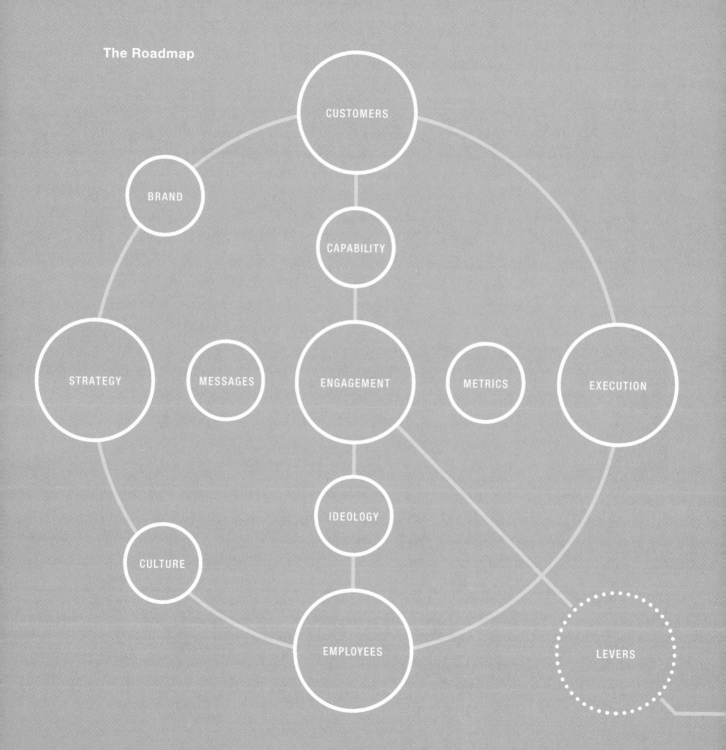

The Roadmap

CUSTOMERS

BRAND

CAPABILITY

STRATEGY

MESSAGES

ENGAGEMENT

METRICS

EXECUTION

IDEOLOGY

CULTURE

EMPLOYEES

LEVERS

© INSIDE RESEARCH

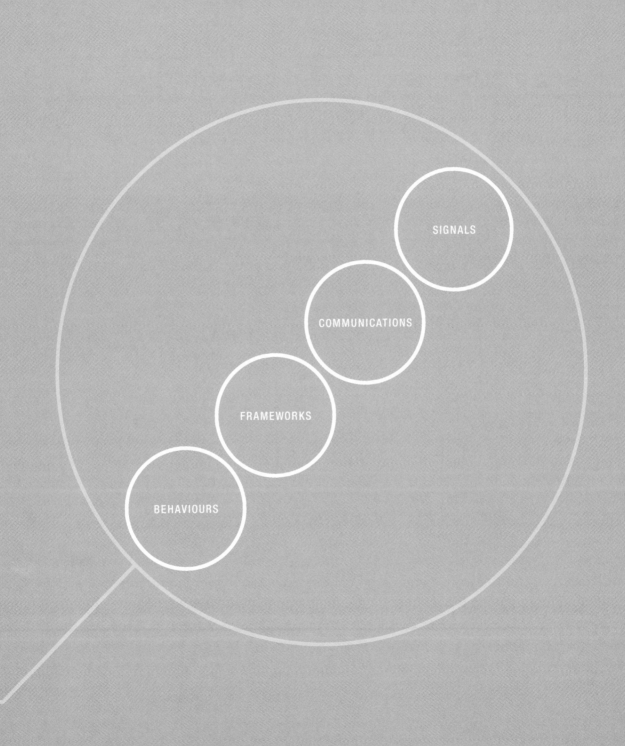

Once the program is up and running, the team cannot afford to ease up on their efforts. They must provide everyone with feedback on how the program is tracking. In addition, the team needs to regularly review and refresh their strategy.

Stage 06//00

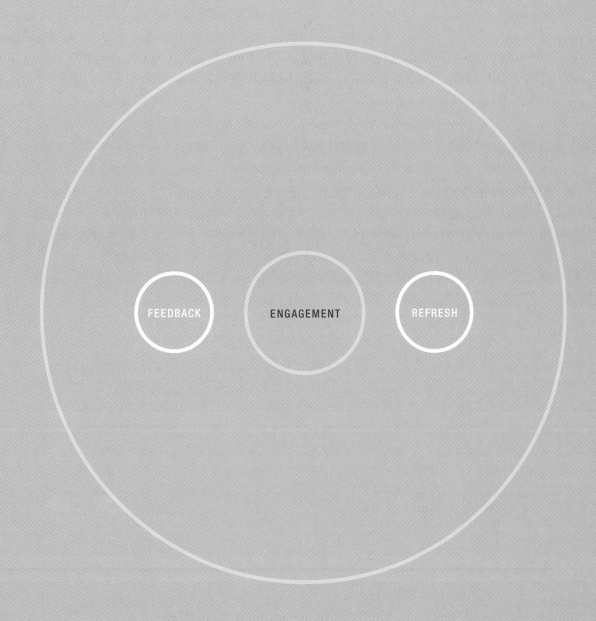

FEEDBACK

ENGAGEMENT

REFRESH

Everybody needs to receive feedback on how the program is progressing. In order to deliver this feedback the engagement team needs to identify their major performance milestones in advance of the program commencing. These milestones should cover three discrete levels inside the business: macro, mini and micro.

Macro milestones are the performance measures for the entire business. These measures are typically wide-ranging and might include, but not be limited to, the organisation's staff engagement scores, the volume of customer complaints and the monthly revenue figures.

Mini milestones are the performance measures for teams. These are similar to the macro milestones, but the results can be broken down so teams can identify and address specific performance issues inside their part of the business.

And lastly, micro milestones are the performance measures for individual employees. These normally include a mix of hard and soft measures — "What did you achieve?" and "How did you achieve it?".

A company-wide conversation regarding the firm's progress against these measures helps employees to gauge how they, their team and the business are performing. This approach helps to create a *'line of sight'* that enables people to see the link between their work and the organisation's plans and objectives.

At a senior level, the leadership team will want to see evidence that the program is working. Their ultimate objective — if they're managing a listed company — is to increase total shareholder returns. Consequently, the engagement team needs to show how the program is helping the business to achieve this goal.

This requires the preparation of a detailed report on the non-financial drivers of performance, which will typically contain data on employee commitment and productivity, customer loyalty and advocacy, and other important lead indicators such as brand health. The skill is in making sure the system is robust. If it is, improvements in the areas of employee commitment and customer loyalty will inexorably work their way through the system until they reveal themselves on the organisation's bottom line.

IDENTIFY MILESTONES

COMPANY

MACRO

TEAM

MINI

INDIVIDUAL

MICRO

LINK TO THE BOTTOM LINE

ACTION POINTS

#01: Provide everyone with regular feedback on how the program is progressing
#02: Integrate this feedback in the performance management system
#03: Prepare a report that addresses the non-financial drivers of performance

Once the program is up and running, it is tempting for the engagement team to switch on the cruise control. The plan has been prepared, solid foundations set down, what else could there be for them to do?

It is almost inevitable that the workforce — including the leadership team — will start to lose interest in the engagement program at some point.

Often it is the case that a new issue appears on the horizon. The CEO decides to redirect resources, and without the necessary funds in place the program begins to fade into the background. Even if it doesn't happen this way, engagement fatigue tends to set in after two or three years. The human capital indicators on the leadership team's dashboard begin to dip, and the naysayers again question the value of the program.

Developing the initiative as a peripheral component to the day-to-day running of the business is a fundamental error. The program needs to become, "The way we do things around here," rather than a temporary intrusion on normal operations.

The majority of engagement interventions should be hard-wired into the business so they become standard procedure. The sharing of corporate strategy with employees, the development of workforce capability and the relentless simplifying of overly complex systems are all examples of engagement interventions that should become permanent fixtures within the business.

One of the keys to gaining this level of integration is to link the development of the engagement strategy with the development of the corporate strategy. Every year, the leadership team sits down to re-evaluate and refresh their corporate strategy.

Executives who are responsible for developing their organisation's engagement strategy need to synchronise their efforts with this event. Adopting this approach will ensure the objectives of the engagement program are always in alignment with those set out in the main corporate strategy document.

This is a simple solution to a perennial problem. How can executives *'maintain the rage'* for employee engagement? Not just next year, but five and ten years down the track? The answer is to weave the engagement program into the fabric of the business.

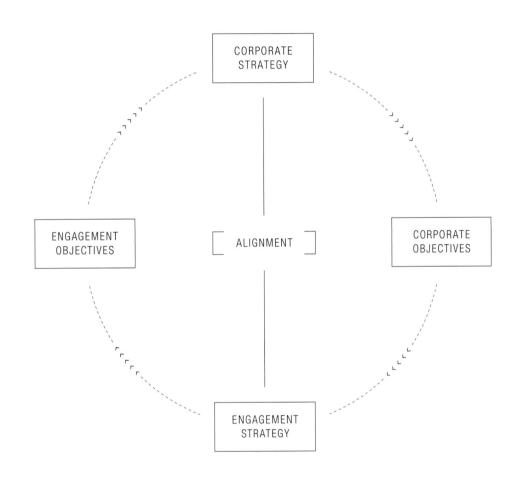

ACTION POINTS

#01: Review the engagement strategy — align it with the corporate strategy
#02: Refresh the program's tactics, themes and tools
#03: Weave the engagement program into the fabric of the business

CHAPTER 8

Success Stories

In researching this book I was fortunate enough to conduct a number of interviews with executives whose organisations have enjoyed success in this area. Real-life case histories and examples help us to understand the practice behind the theory. Looking at what did and didn't work inside another business provides us with priceless lessons from which we can learn.

However, it is a mistake to simply copy another organisation's engagement strategy. Companies are unique and complex organisms. What works successfully in one company or environment commonly falters in another.

To circumvent this potential problem, I decided not to recount an organisation's entire engagement strategy. Instead, I asked the executives I interviewed to talk about one particular aspect of their firm's engagement program. This delivered dual benefits. One, it enabled these executives to openly discuss their experiences without fear they were revealing their company's valuable intellectual property. And two, it ensured this book wasn't presenting a template for others to misguidedly copy.

Two things stood out in my conversations.

First, the dramatic difference in the way each company approached the task of engaging their employees. They adopted similar tools and tactics, but at no stage did I feel they were using the same strategy. This is reassuring; it suggests Australian companies are doing the hard yards up front, developing bespoke engagement strategies that are appropriate for their business, culture and people.

...engaging employees is not only the right thing to do but from a business point of view, it's the smart thing to do.

Second, the passion and commitment of the executives I interviewed was palpable. These people are ardent advocates of employee engagement. They genuinely believe that engaging employees is not only the right thing to do but from a business point of view, it's the smart thing to do. This too is reassuring; it suggests these executives are embracing employee engagement as a business tool rather than the latest fad *'du jour'.*

The tone of the interviews is deliberately informal. My intention was to relate a sense of what each company was doing, rather than attempting to describe in detail the exact steps taken. Finally, I believe the content of these interviews clearly signal the enormous potential of this new management tool to attract, motivate and retain employees.

- ANZ Bank: Cultural Transformation
- Stockland: *'Our Voice'* Employee Survey
- KPMG Australia: *People First* Program
- Unilever Australia: Volunteering Program
- CSC Australia: The *'Get Aligned'* Initiative
- AMP: Leadership Frameworks
- Vodafone Australia: *'Red, Rock Solid and Restless'*
- St George Bank: Workforce Capability
- Mallesons Stephen Jaques: Mentoring Program

ANZ BANK

Cultural Transformation

One of the best known cultural transformation programs in Australia is ANZ's *Breakout* program. It was back in 2000 that the ANZ leadership team started on its long journey to build a business that was both high performing and values-driven. The background to the *Breakout* program and the initiatives the leadership team developed and implemented make a fascinating story. However, much of this information has already been well reported on — and readers who want to know more can find an overview of the program on ANZ's website at *www.anz.com.*

Sitting down with Shane Freeman, ANZ's General Manager of People Capital and Breakout, was an opportunity to explore his views on what does and doesn't work when it comes to building engagement levels inside one of this country's top 20 companies.

The easygoing Freeman thinks we need to do all we can to take the mystique out of employee engagement. He likes to use a simple framework when he looks at the topic.

As he sees it, human beings are a mass of contradictions. "On one level we're extremely complex, and at another level, our core needs are virtually identical across the planet." Identify and tap into these needs and, in Freeman's opinion, you'll hit a sweet spot every time. He believes we have four basic needs, and whether or not these needs are met plays a major role in shaping the experience we have while we are at work.

Freeman explains that the first need we have is for security. "If you can get people to feel secure inside the workplace it opens them up. So we spend a lot of time in this organisation trying to give people a sense of security, so they can contribute without fear."

"It's not about money; it's about your boss or your peers genuinely acknowledging your effort."

One of the ways the bank tries to do this is through its *Breakout* workshops. These are two- and three-day personal development courses that teach people how to have open and honest conversations with each other. This in turn helps to build the levels of trust inside the business, which directly feeds into whether or not people feel secure. "Once they do, they can flourish and be their best," says Freeman.

The second need we have is for our work to feel important. Each of us needs to feel that it makes a difference whether or not we turn up for work in the morning. Freeman believes that accountability is important in this space. "We have a devolved operating model where the balance of power lies with the divisions and business units in ANZ," he says. "We push the decision-making capability closer to the pointy end of the business, closer to the customer." This approach gives ANZ's employees a chance to contribute, and work out what is and isn't important, enabling them to make decisions and make a difference. When people are given the opportunity to do this, they know what they do matters, not only to them, but to their manager and colleagues.

The third need we have is for recognition. "People need to know that they're more than a number." Freeman believes this extrinsic recognition is crucial. "While it's great to know yourself that you're kicking goals, that what you're doing is actually moving the dial, it can feel a bit hollow if no one else notices." The great bosses know this, and they deliberately set out to provide their people with regular pats on the back. "It's not about money; it's about your boss or your peers genuinely acknowledging your effort."

He believes that leaders and managers need to continually look for ways to stretch their people.

The fourth and final need we have is to feel that we're growing and developing. "You can have all of your other needs met, but if you don't feel you're growing and developing, you begin to switch off and there's not much engagement in that," says Freeman. He believes that leaders and managers need to continually look for ways to stretch their people. It might be working on a new product, or developing a new skill, or discovering something about themself that they never knew, but when people get a chance to learn and grow the whole experience keeps them alert and interested.

Freeman recognises that he's making this task sound a lot simpler than it is, but he feels that it is far too easy to overcomplicate this subject, "All we've tried to do with the *Breakout* program is put in place some processes, structures and symbols that encourage people to have the conversations that I'm talking about." If the people inside an organisation start to recognise and address each other's needs, then real progress can begin to be made in the areas of employee satisfaction and engagement.

Another area that Freeman believes has made an important contribution to ANZ's success in the area of workplace engagement is the ongoing measurement of the organisation's values.

This is a unique aspect to the bank's people and culture strategy. Each year, for the last seven years, the bank has surveyed its staff using Cultural Transformation Tools' *Values Assessment Survey*. This survey asks staff to select ten values from a long list of 100, that best describe:

- The culture they currently experience at the bank
- The organisational culture they'd like to work in
- Their top ten personal values

Back in 2000, the results from the survey showed that ANZ employees didn't think much of the bank's culture, selecting words such as *'bureaucracy'*, *'hierarchical'*, *'long hours'* and *'risk-aversion'* to describe it. To add to the general sense of malaise on this issue, staff saw little or no alignment between the bank's culture and their own values.

Freeman recalls that it was the disappointing results from this research that provided the leadership team with the ammunition it needed to begin doing something about this problem. This in turn led to the launch of the *Perform, Grow and Breakout* strategy.

Seven years down the track, this groundbreaking strategy has enabled the bank's culture to undergo a radical transformation. The table overleaf shows in detail the progression of cultural change over the last seven years.

It's remarkable to look at the values selected in 2000 and see how universally negative they were, and then to compare them with the values chosen by staff in 2007. The top five values inside the business now clearly reflect the interests of the bank's external stakeholders — customers, shareholders and the community. The negative values — those with the letter (L) next to them on the table — that were a major element in the original survey have completely disappeared.

This table shows the shifts in perception of ANZ's culture over the period 2000–07.

(L) = Limiting value

Values Assessment Survey by Corporate Transformation Tools

	2000	2002
01	Cost reduction	Cost reduction
02	Profit	Customer focus
03	Shareholder value	Shareholder value
04	Accountability	Accountability
05	Continuous improvement	Continuous improvement
06	Customer focus	Profit
07	Bureaucracy (L)	Results orientation
08	Achievement	Achievement
09	Goals orientation	Community involvement
10	Heirarchical (L)	Customer satisfaction
11	Short term focus (L)	Teamwork
12	Long hours (L)	Being the best
13	Commitment	Organisational growth
14	Risk-averse (L)	Bureaucracy (L)
15		Balance (home/work)
16		Long hours (L)
17		Productivity
18		Brand image
19		Heirarchical (L)
20		Can do approach
21		

2004–5	2006	2007	$\circ$
Customer focus	Profit	Customer satisfaction	01
Community involvement	Customer focus	Customer focus	02
Cost reduction	Community involvement	Profit	03
Accountability	Accountability	Community involvement	04
Results orientation	Organisational growth	Results orientation	05
Brand image	Achievement	Brand image	06
Achievement	Brand image	Shareholder value	07
Profit	Results orientation	Accountability	08
Bureaucracy (L)	Shareholder value	Organisational growth	09
Customer satisfaction	Cost reduction	Teamwork	10
Continuous improvement	Customer satisfaction	Achievement	11
Shareholder value	Being the best	Cost reduction	12
Teamwork	Teamwork	Being the best	13
Being the best	Perform	Staff engagement	14
Balance (home/work)	Balance (home/work)	Risk conscious	15
Perform	Continuous improvement	Balance (home/work)	16
Best practice	Best practice	Values driven	17
Long hours (L)	Professionalism	Diversity	18
Organisational growth	Productivity	Continuous improvement	19
Hierarchical (L)	Risk-averse (L)	Social responsibility	20
		Making a difference	21

With the benefit of hindsight, Freeman can now identify individual events inside the bank that shifted values up or down the ladder. "*'Community involvement'* is a good example of this. In 2002 it was sitting way back in ninth position on the ladder, but in our 2004–05 survey it leapt up into second place. And the big kick on this was the Boxing Day Tsunami. We didn't realise it at the time, but staff really took notice of the way we opened up our contact centre to the organisations who were trying to raise aid for the victims of this terrible disaster."

Freeman also recalls how results from one survey shaped management's thinking on a key issue. "A hiring freeze in 2004 led to the unwanted reappearance of *'bureaucracy'* in our top ten values in the subsequent survey period. This was our people letting us know in certain terms that they were unhappy we didn't trust them to make the right call on balancing head count and revenue. The leadership team learnt from this and we agreed it was an approach we wouldn't use again."

Freeman says he views the *Values Assessment Survey* — which is now part of the bank's annual *Engagement and Culture Survey* — as a finely tuned instrument that accurately reflects what is going on inside the business and how ANZ's employees are experiencing the organisation. "I now look at it as a lead indicator. What we see in the values survey tends to show up a year later on the engagement survey."

The last issue Freeman raises is perhaps the most controversial. He believes management teams can fall into the trap of relying too heavily on programs to improve

"What we see in the values survey tends to show up a year later on the engagement survey."

their organisation's engagement scores. "What a score of sixty-odd per cent on an engagement survey is telling us is that we've got forty-odd per cent of our people who, for some reason, are saying they're not going to check to the right of a couple of critical questions on engagement," he says. "If I try and fix this problem solely with programs I'm taking the heat off our managers and that's a mistake because it's managers who determine whether or not people are engaged. You can have all these great programs in place but if your boss isn't giving you the four things that I talked about earlier, then a program isn't going to make any difference."

Freeman believes one of the most powerful things the bank has done in this space is to remove the focus from the program and instead put the emphasis on what the numbers are really saying, which is, "There are three or four people in every team of ten who aren't engaged and as a leader or manager you need to know who they are, what their issues are, and what you can do to address them."

His own solution to this problem is to sit down with the people in his team and have an open and honest discussion about what they are thinking and feeling. He uses Hewitt's *'Say, Stay and Strive'* model to begin a peer-to-peer conversation that gives him a sense of where this person is really at, what's working for them and what's not working so well. "You need to make this personal," he says. "People need to know you've got a genuine interest in their welfare, and all you're trying to establish is what it is that you or the business need to start doing to ensure they'll score higher next time."

...this transformation has generated quantifiable results that are truly impressive.

The *Breakout* program has brought about a huge cultural transformation inside the bank. And as mentioned previously in this book, this transformation has generated quantifiable results that are truly impressive. The bank's engagement scores, customer satisfaction figures and financial results all combine to provide irrefutable evidence of the benefits that can be derived from adopting a *'people-first'* approach.

STOCKLAND

'Our Voice' Employee Survey

Stockland is the largest diversified property group in Australia. With a market capitalisation of over $11 billion and assets in excess of $13 billion, this is a substantial business that has managed to generate over 25 consecutive years of profit growth for its shareholders.

One look at this organisation's employee engagement score and it immediately becomes apparent that it's the people who work inside this business who are the driving force behind this stellar performance. Sitting at an impressively high 85 per cent — which positions Stockland in the top quartile of Towers Perrin-ISR's *Global High Performing Companies Norm* — the survey result confirms that Stockland's employees are among the most engaged on the planet.[18]

This suggests that entering Stockland's *'Vertical Village'* in Sydney's CBD to meet Chris Akayan, General Manager of Organisational Development and Richard Laidlaw, Group Manager of Learning & Development will be an opportunity to discover the magic formula to generating employee engagement.

Disappointingly, both Akayan and Laidlaw are quick to dispel this notion. "Although we have a history of surveying our people, we only formally began using the Towers Perrin-ISR employee engagement survey in 2005," explains Akayan. "What we were fortunate to find was that we already had in place many of what I describe as the organisational building blocks of employee engagement."

According to Akayan, a management team needs three building blocks in position if it wants to generate engagement. One, your people need to feel they are part of a winning team. Two, you need to provide every employee with work they find meaningful and challenging. And three, the leadership team needs to convince everyone inside the business that they are genuinely interested in their wellbeing.

"When you run your first survey, you've got to appreciate that every organisation will be at a certain level, and that might be really high or low, but all the data does is tell you where you are," says Akayan. "So when we conducted our first survey and scored 82 per cent, that was because we already had our foundations in place. And what we have done over the last couple of years is build on these foundations by making our leaders more accessible and by doing a lot of work around issues like leadership development and performance management."

Laidlaw picks up on this theme "Where there is a high engagement score, it is often a reflection of a lack of interference from management. We are always looking at what we can do to get things out of people's way, so they can be who they really want to be, in a place where they really like being and go on a journey that they find really exciting."

As the conversation progresses it becomes clear that Stockland's *'Our Voice'* Employee Survey plays a key role in identifying what is *'getting in the way'* of the people inside this organisation. Containing over 150 questions, the survey covers a wide range of topics and issues, including: values, customer focus, performance planning, leadership, communication, learning and development — over 15 different subject headings in total.

"The survey results determine what we are going to focus on in the year ahead," says

"Where there is a high engagement score, it is often a reflection of a lack of interference from management."

Akayan. "It's data-driven rather than trend-driven. We concentrate on what our people are telling us and make sure we address the problems that the numbers highlight."

It is the attention to detail in creating the staff survey and then unpacking and understanding the resulting data that marks out Stockland's approach. This isn't an annual or bi-annual box-ticking event; it is integral to the way this business operates.

The starting point for the process is deciding what questions will go into the survey. Akayan says it's important that most of the survey remains static from year-to-year, in order to track trends over time and benchmark the organisation's performance against Australian companies and global norms. "However, we can explore specific issues if we want to. For example, last year we asked our people, 'What originally attracted you to Stockland?' and 'What keeps you here?' Then we gave them a list of 12 items to choose from and it was interesting to see the differences between what attracted them and what keeps them here, but also to see what they put as 1, 2 and 3 as opposed to 10, 11, and 12." But Akayan emphasises that it is the core of the survey which drives and shapes the agenda for the year ahead.

Once the content of the survey is finalised, it goes out into the business. In the past Stockland has run a combination of online and paper-based surveys to accommodate those who were unable to access a computer. However, the business now conducts a single online survey, a fact that doesn't seem to have harmed the participation rate that sits at a lofty 91 per cent. "We are confident the survey gives us the right numbers

*"So we don't just look at the data;
we make sure we get the story
behind it as well."*

because of the high response rate we get," says Laidlaw. "So for us the survey is not a sample. It's more like a census."

As soon as they receive the survey data back from Towers Perrin-ISR, the entire business pores over the numbers. "Typically, what happens is that Matthew Quinn, our Managing Director, and the Executive Committee allocate a few hours to go through the results immediately after they are available," says Akayan. "Then we do a presentation to the Board and they are always very interested in the results and key messages. After that, the leadership team of each business unit attends a debrief session and then there are further debrief and action planning sessions at a team level."

Laidlaw explains that in terms of action planning, there are some things that need to be taken care of at a group level, for example, making adjustments to the performance management system, or the group's approach to career development planning. And then there are things that are applicable at a business unit level, where the survey has highlighted a particular issue in one part of the business, or one business has received a low score on an individual question. That area of the business then runs an action planning meeting that is relevant to that problem, so they can address it and fix it.

When asked to provide an example of how this process works, Laidlaw recalls that the remuneration system showed up as a problem in a recent survey. "What we discovered was that the remuneration system was more opaque than we would have liked. The survey told us that our people were unclear about how their total pay was arrived at. So within weeks we reacted and designed a communication message that explained our remuneration system on one page, so everyone knew the level they were at — we have five or six levels — and at every level it was very clear how each individual's pay package fitted together with their short-term incentive and how it fitted together for others. So we worked on clearing up any misunderstanding and got a seven-point increase in the pay section of the next survey."

This level of understanding is a result of a deliberate decision by Stockland to always look for the narrative behind the numbers. Laidlaw explains that they make sure to have lots of dialogue sessions with the people who complete the survey. "So we don't just look at the data; we make sure we get the story behind it as well. And this helps us to clearly identify the issues that sit behind a certain score, providing us with insights that may not have been obvious if we were just looking at the data on its own."

The business also uses the survey to assess the performance of its leaders. "The survey gives us an engagement score and a *People Leader Index* which is an assessment of a leader by all those people who are in their team, and both of these numbers hook into an individual's bonus. This has helped us integrate the survey into the business as part of management's scorecard," says Akayan. "It is now an operational activity as opposed to an HR activity. In some companies, they do the survey but it doesn't connect back to the remuneration system, the learning agenda or what's happening inside the business. It's disconnected and because of that, the impact is diluted."

"…it's absolutely crucial to have leaders who want to own the engagement issue…"

Akayan acknowledges that it's absolutely crucial to have leaders who want to own the engagement issue if a business is to achieve this level of integration. "The leaders here have absolutely accepted the idea that the engagement survey is one of the most powerful tools they have at their disposal," he says. "We deliver the survey and facilitate the process of cascading it through the organisation, but it's the involvement and commitment of our leaders that ensures the actions and strategies we adopt make a real difference."

After the meeting, there is an opportunity to flick through Stockland's recently published, *Corporate Responsibility and Sustainability Summary Report.*[19] The report provides specific quantifiable evidence of the value that Stockland's employees place on their leadership and workplace culture. Of respondents surveyed:

- 95 per cent feel proud to work at Stockland
- 97 per cent are willing to work beyond what is required in their job to help Stockland succeed and
- 95 per cent say they fully support the values for which Stockland stands

These responses suggest that there is much we can learn from studying Stockland's approach to generating employee engagement. Perhaps they have discovered the magic formula after all!

KPMG AUSTRALIA

People First Program

KPMG is a global network of professional firms providing audit, tax and advisory services to a largely blue-chip client base. In Australia, the firm operates across 14 offices with over 300 partners and 4,000 people.

For organisations like KPMG, the only sustainable competitive advantage they have rests in the quality of the people who go up and down in the firm's lifts every day. If KPMG is unable to attract and retain the best and brightest talent in the marketplace its future success is in jeopardy. This is a risk of which James Allt-Graham, National Managing Partner of People, Performance and Culture at KPMG is all too aware. In setting the scene for a discussion of KPMG's *People First* program, Allt-Graham goes back to 2005 to highlight some of the problems confronting the firm that led to the development of this groundbreaking initiative.

"The business had in place some ambitious growth targets for 2010 and we knew what that meant in terms of headcount growth," explains Allt-Graham. "The problem was we were going to have to grow our workforce in a much tighter labour market, with fewer graduates to choose from and an increasingly competitive market for lateral hires. On top of this, we could see from our staff turnover figures that the firm was churning through people at an unsustainable rate."

The other thing that happened at about this time was that the firm received back the numbers from its engagement survey, and it's fair to say that the results weren't encouraging. Allt-Graham notes, "There were a couple of areas in the survey where we were pretty disappointed with our performance, so these results in combination with the demands of our growth strategy led us to say, 'Right, we've got to do something fundamentally different about how we're managing our people'."

This was where the *People First* strategy was born, with the objective of creating an environment in which KPMG's people could flourish and realise their full potential. In early 2005, the firm appointed Peter Nash as the first National Managing Partner of People, Performance and Culture — the position now occupied by Allt-Graham. Nash's appointment was a clear signal to everyone inside the firm that attraction and retention was a priority issue for the National Executive Committee. "Managing people and getting this agenda right was absolutely front and centre to the decisions that we made, and continue to make at an executive level and through the business," says Allt-Graham.

"Over the last couple of years there have been five key areas that we've been building on," he says. "Leadership, diversity and flexibility, recognition and reward, career development and performance management, and much of our work has been about setting the policies and making sure we've the right infrastructure in place."

The first element of the program that Allt-Graham mentions is leadership, but this is not the expected conversation on leadership development. Instead, he explains how the firm has created an infrastructure that cascades accountability for the program through the business. "On the leadership side we instituted the People, Performance and Culture (PPC) structure," he says. "Within each of our major divisions and each of

"…much of our work has been about setting the policies and making sure we've the right infrastructure in place."

our major geographies we have a PPC Executive Partner. These are senior partners who are accountable for driving the people agenda within their business and down to the next level. At that next level we have PPC Partners who are responsible for leading the agenda within their business unit. And then we drive down to what we call our community groups, which are groups of eight to ten employees and each of these has a partner who takes responsibility for that group."

It is clear that this firm-wide commitment to the *People First* program is the difference between mouthing platitudes on issues like employee satisfaction and engagement, and doing something tangible and meaningful about it. "It is through this structure that most of our messaging and policies hit the road," says Allt-Graham. "Partners are responsible for the people inside their group and they report monthly on key metrics such as turnover and the completion of performance and career management processes."

The second element of the *People First* program that Allt-Graham raises is diversity and flexibility; a subject that the firm takes very seriously.

The number of flexible work options KPMG offers its staff is staggering and includes: variation to hours, part-time work, job sharing, working from home, career breaks and gradual re-entry or exit arrangements. Allt-Graham shrewdly notes that, "On the flexibility side it's easy to issue policies about job sharing and enabling people to work part-time, but what you need is a culture where a person feels they can ask to use these policies. So we've had a big focus on trying to increase people's take up rates in these areas

"It's much better for the firm to have three-fifths or four-fifths of someone who's really good than not have them at all."

and pleasingly we've seen a 23 per cent increase in flexible work arrangements over the last two years." Allt-Graham also emphasises the importance of having role models in place to encourage take up. "We have female partners in particular who've come on as part-time partners who are important role models in this area. To go back even five or six years and to be entered into partnership on a part-time basis was unheard of. It is now common practice and for us as a business, it's fantastic. It's much better for the firm to have three-fifths or four-fifths of someone who's really good than not have them at all." And Allt-Graham points out that it's not just women who are making the most of these new policies. "We've single fathers and other people in the firm who, from a work-life balance perspective, are choosing to work three or four days a week."

The subject of diversity is one that Allt-Graham is clearly passionate about. "For us diversity is about understanding and embracing difference, which is important when you consider the cultural and ethnic diversity of the people inside this firm."

KPMG recently completed its first diversity survey, which provided the firm with some very positive feedback but also some clear issues it needs to address. "For example, we need to be sensitive to small things such as when we schedule conferences, looking at a religious calendar," he says. "Does the chosen date impact on a particular group? Is there anything we can do to prevent this from being a problem?"

One interesting initiative that Allt-Graham mentions is the introduction of prayer rooms in all of KPMG's major offices over Ramadan. "The firm has a fairly low percentage of Muslims relative to the total population, but the feedback we got back from providing the prayer rooms was very positive," he says. "The people who used the rooms didn't feel they had to duck into an office, or leave the building to pray. We provided them with a facility and it showed that the firm respected and understood their needs."

But KPMG doesn't view diversity as just a gender, religious or cultural issue. "For example, we've gone through all of our policies on sexual orientation to make sure they're non-discriminatory," says Allt-Graham. "So if a gay couple chooses to move interstate, they get the same benefits as a married couple. We've made sure there is no hidden bias in our policy framework in terms of sexual orientation and that's an area we will continue to focus on in the future."

The third strand to the *People First* program is reward and recognition. The reward aspect of the program entails making sure the firm's salary and benefits packages are competitive. Part of this work involves formalising the bonus framework and making sure that the profit share scheme and discretionary bonus scheme are consistent and transparent. "One thing people hate is inconsistency, so we've been working really hard on getting these elements right," says Allt-Graham.

The benefits package KPMG offers its people recognises that an individual's needs and aspirations will change over their working life. This has resulted in the development of a range of benefits that emphasise choice and flexibility — annual health assessments, professional counselling, international assignments, the payment of professional fees, in fact a seemingly never-ending list of opportunities and benefits — which allows individuals to choose a package that works for them.

The recognition aspect of the program looks at the non-financial rewards the business offers its staff. Allt-Graham mentions that the 2004 *Global People Survey* provided clear feedback that people inside the firm didn't feel appreciated. "Recognition, even if it was given, was often late," he says. "What we've been focusing on is making sure that when people have been working hard or doing a great job, we take the time to say well done."

The fourth component of the *People First* program that Allt-Graham highlights is career development; people need to know they have a future with the firm. To address this issue, the business has developed career maps that take people through the transitions from graduate to senior partner. These maps help people to have a conversation with their manager about what they want to do and where they want to go. "Maybe I don't want to stay in the advisory business or the audit business, I want to move into tax, so it enables people to look at different career paths and plan their development," says Allt-Graham. "And of course this links into our learning and development framework and our performance management framework, which is another example of how we've developed the infrastructure so we can push solutions down to the frontline."

The last element of the program Allt-Graham raises is performance management. KPMG has in place a comprehensive system that takes into account the non-financial aspects of performance; more of a balanced scorecard approach. "What we are seeing

> *"We're not just talking about this issue, we're actually driving it with incentives as well."*

right now is people being promoted or receiving bonuses based on really outstanding contributions around managing people," he says. "We're not just talking about this issue, we're actually driving it with incentives as well."

A lot of businesses make the mistake of hesitating over creating this link between performance and people. Employees want to see how the business treats leaders who make their numbers, but for some reason fail their people. Do they still receive a bonus? Do they still get a promotion? Or are they penalised? "That's a tough conversation, so part of our leadership development is around helping people to have far more open and honest communication around these sorts of performance issues," says Allt-Graham.

The results KPMG has achieved on the back of this program are impressive. The headcount has increased from 3,375 to 4,100. Employee turnover has dropped from 20.3 per cent to 15.8 per cent. The firm's staff engagement score has increased from 76 per cent to 83 per cent, leading the business to reset its benchmark from the Towers Perrin-ISR *Professional Services Norm* to the *High Performance Norm*, a result of which Allt-Graham says, the firm is particularly proud. On top of this, the business is achieving double-digit revenue growth, a sure sign that its *People First* strategy is hitting the mark.

When asked what lies ahead, Allt-Graham's response is, "We've got our policies and frameworks in place, so now we need to make sure they become part of the way we do things. They're not an afterthought, they're not something we do off to the side but they're absolutely central to the way we do business."

...what is most notable is the scope and scale of the exercise.

A few days later, and with time to reflect on the *People First* program, what is most notable is the scope and scale of the exercise. The People, Performance and Culture Unit left no stone unturned as it set about the task of delivering the people at KPMG a more satisfying and rewarding work experience. It is a perfect example of the level of effort leadership teams need to put into attracting, engaging and retaining their people.

UNILEVER AUSTRALIA

Volunteering Program

At first glance, it can seem surprising that employee volunteering is a cornerstone of most, if not all, large-scale engagement initiatives. Why do so many organisations use volunteering programs to generate engagement? It's because they're so effective at reaching those areas of the engagement matrix that are notoriously difficult to access.

A well-planned employer-sponsored volunteering program can lift staff satisfaction scores and contribute to the retention of employees by satisfying the need we all have for meaning and purpose in our lives. Working towards and contributing to something bigger than ourselves engenders positive emotions and these emotions invariably affect how we feel about the organisation we work for. We feel good about doing good.

The global brands giant Unilever developed its program during a period of turbulent change for the business. Nick Goddard, Corporate Relations Director at Unilever Australia, who lead the development and implementation of the program, takes up the story. "As part of a strategic plan to refine our brand portfolio, we had to divest ourselves of a large number of businesses and brands. While employees understood the need for this action and supported it, it left them feeling understandably anxious," he explains. "We saw an opportunity to address this issue by establishing a community-focused volunteering program that would galvanise employees during this difficult period."

Goddard developed the program with two key insights in mind. Firstly, he knew if he wanted a high participation rate, he would need to consult with employees to determine which issues they thought the business should tackle. This would ensure employees felt they were part of the solution, which is crucial if you want to generate engagement off the back of this type of work. Secondly, he didn't want this to just be a cheque-signing exercise. Anything the business did would have to involve employees getting out there, getting their hands dirty and contributing in a real and tangible way.

To determine exactly what to do, Goddard engaged a consultancy to organise employee discussion groups around the business. Each group commenced with the challenge: "We want to invest in the communities around us. We've got the money to do that, but we want your help to identify the areas into which we should direct this money. All the participants in the groups were very forthcoming with their ideas, two of which really stood out," recalls Goddard. "The first idea evolved into our successful *World of Work* program, which provides the long-term unemployed with the guidance and support that they need to re-enter the workforce. The second idea, of addressing children's literacy problems, was much harder to bring to life. While there's no question literacy is important, how could we get employees to make a worthwhile contribution in this area?"

To address this issue Unilever ended up partnering with an organisation called Learning Links, a not-for-profit organisation that helps children with learning difficulties. "They helped us to develop *Reading for Life*, a 14-week program designed for children in primary school who need help with their reading," says Goddard. "Learning Links identified the schools that would take part in the program and trained our volunteers, ensuring they felt well prepared and confident about what they were doing."

...other businesses unrelated to Unilever have begun to use the same model in different schools around the country.

At the school, the volunteers *'buddy up'* with a child for 45 minutes each week, for a period of just over three months. They follow a program that is designed to encourage the child to realise their reading potential and, in doing so, develop self-confidence. "It's not just about sitting down next to a child and correcting them as they read; that would be self-defeating, as the child who already has a reading problem is now asked to read in front of a strange adult and is corrected as they go," explains Goddard. "Instead, the program involves interactive board games and the learning of sight words and phonemics in a fun and interesting way. The idea is to make sure the child enjoys the experience, which makes it more likely that they'll learn."

Goddard says the results have exceeded everyone's expectations. Pre- and post-testing has shown that the program has made a significant difference to the average reading age of the kids who participated. Comprehension levels have improved by an average of eight months, reading accuracy by an average of seven months and reading fluency by an average of five months. In fact, the program has proven so successful that other businesses unrelated to Unilever have begun to use the same model in different schools around the country.

"Being able to obtain hard measures also enabled us to communicate to our volunteers, and the rest of the team here at Unilever, the impact that their efforts were having," says Goddard. "Contributing your time is one thing, but knowing you are truly and tangibly making a difference to someone else's life, that really is something very special."

"The truly remarkable thing is that everybody benefits from this approach."

As Goddard concludes, "The truly remarkable thing is that everybody benefits from this approach. Employees enjoy the *'feel good'* factor generated by contributing to a worthwhile cause. The children in the program receive support and assistance that would otherwise be unavailable. And we, as an organisation, derive the benefits that flow from having a more satisfied and engaged workforce."

CSC AUSTRALIA

The *'Get Aligned'* Initiative

CSC Australia (CSC) is a wholly owned subsidiary of Computer Sciences Corporation, a US$16.1 billion global giant that provides its clients with a mix of services including systems integration, IT outsourcing and consulting. In Australia, the business employs over 3,300 people located across 50 offices. Local clients include well-known names such as BHP Billiton, AMP, Coles, Rio Tinto and QBE.

Over the past few years, CSC has undergone a transformation that has fundamentally changed the way it is organised and run. The results are remarkable; with the business recording its best ever performance in terms of employee engagement, customer satisfaction and financial results.

The seeds for this story were sown back in 2003 when CSC found itself confronting challenges on all sides. Externally, customers' expectations were shifting rapidly; those who weren't sending their work to the sub-continent were demanding far more innovation and value from their IT partners. Internally, the situation was no better. Financial performance was lacklustre, employees were disengaged after a long period of cost cutting and the executive team lacked cohesion.

Leanne McDonald, Director of Organisational Development and Learning at CSC picks up the story: "It was around this time that our CEO, Mike Shove and his executive team began looking at their leadership style. They understood that as long as they kept doing the same thing they were going to get the same results."

As the team explored the use of a more constructive and collaborative style of leadership it became apparent that the business lacked a clear and compelling vision for employees to rally around. McDonald sets this in context when she explains, "Traditionally this business spent most of its time doing budget planning, not strategic planning. We were great at operational efficiency, but that wasn't going to get us to where we wanted to be. We needed a new vision."

McDonald recalls management had three value propositions to choose from when it sat down to define CSC's new mission and vision — product innovation, operational efficiency or customer intimacy. "The executive team said, 'We're not product innovators, we're not getting the growth we need from operational efficiency, but customer intimacy is an area where we are already strong and it's something our employees can relate to'." The new vision was crystallised as *'CSC Australia will be No.1 in Customer Intimacy'.*

Shove and his team set about developing a new corporate strategy that would provide the business with a roadmap to realising this vision.

The executive team built the new strategy using a balanced scorecard framework — which looks at strategy from four different perspectives: financial, customer, internal processes and learning and growth. At the end of the strategy development process, the team distilled its plan down to a single page strategy map.

McDonald explains that this *'plan on a page'* was a great memory jogger for senior executives. "It neatly connected the company's vision and mission to financial goals, business priorities and key strategic initiatives."

"...the challenge was to engage and align the entire organisation around the vision and the strategy..."

The only problem was that to the uninitiated, the map looked nothing more than a mass of colourful circles, randomly connected by some squiggly lines. McDonald acknowledges this when she says, "Under the learning and growth perspective of this new strategy we had a number of key objectives, one of which was to create an *'engaged and aligned organisation'*. To make that happen we had to take a high-level conceptual document and translate it into something that the average employee sitting in a data centre could understand and act on."

Put simply, the challenge was to engage and align the entire organisation around the vision and the strategy, and link everyone's goals to customer, company and business unit outcomes.

McDonald says, "Some people felt we could send the strategy map out in an email, or present it to staff in a PowerPoint pack. However, the consultants we were working with recommended we use a Root Learning, *Learning Map*® to get our message across."[20]

"A *Learning Map*® is an easy-to-understand, customised learning tool that uses a simple metaphor to draw people into the details of a strategic plan," explains McDonald. "We began using the maps in 2005 and for our first strategy session — *All Aboard* — we adopted the metaphor of a sailing ship setting out on a long voyage. The sails of the ship represented our four different strategy perspectives and there were rocks and navigation aids in our path, and on a distant island you could see a sign that spelled out our vision *'No.1 in Customer Intimacy'* and mission, *'Customers Experience Results'*.

"We had to review our systems and structures if we wanted to engage and align employees around the new strategy."

"Forums were run for 20 to 100 employees at a time," continues McDonald. "People divided up into small groups and joined a table hosted by a table captain. The executive team and senior managers walked everyone through a facilitated strategy session centred on the *Learning Map*®. At appropriate moments the table captains took over and everyone had the chance to ask questions and discuss the issues confronting the business. 'Who do you think our competitors are?' 'What advantages do they hold over us?' 'What are the external forces of change?' The session included group activities and video presentations from our customers, talking candidly about how they saw us."

The strategy briefing sessions were a huge success. Employees who attended received a clear explanation of CSC's new strategy and gained an understanding of their role in bringing the plan to life at an operational level.

McDonald says this was only the starting point. "We had to review our systems and structures if we wanted to engage and align employees around the new strategy."

CEO, Mike Shove cleared the decks by reducing the number of strategic initiatives from a mind-boggling 72 to a more manageable seven, all of which were focused on helping the business realise its *'customer intimacy'* vision.

The business simplified its leadership structure and clarified accountabilities. McDonald notes, "We couldn't expect the executive team to take on the responsibility for implementing every initiative. We created a senior leadership group to drive key strategic initiatives and a strategic project office to monitor and measure progress."

McDonald continues, "Another measure we took was to align all business unit strategies to the new CSC strategy. This allowed leaders and managers to interpret the new strategy into their own world."

On top of this, the business created education programs, aimed at facilitating discussions between leaders and managers and the people on their teams. McDonald recalls, "As an example, we developed a training program for our managers that gave them a refresher on how to translate strategy into business plans for their teams and set meaningful goals for their people."

The results from this work were very positive. Customers noticed an improvement in service, employee morale went up and the business began hitting its financial targets. The icing on the cake was CSC's HR team receiving the Australian Human Resources Institute's award for *Excellence in People Management* for its work on this initiative.

The following year the goal alignment initiative was refreshed — and officially dubbed 'Get Aligned'. The *Learning Map*® was updated and given a new theme, *Sailing to Success*. McDonald says, "It was a celebration of success, showing everyone how much progress we'd made, but also emphasising how we'd only just started on this long journey."

Again, McDonald and her team did a huge amount of work behind the scenes, developing tools and programs that would help the business to vertically align around the plan. The aim was for goals to swiftly flow down through the business to the people at the coalface.

One of the most impressive pieces of work McDonald describes is a goal alignment model. "We realised we needed to do more work to help individuals align their goals. We are a global company with multiple stakeholders who all have competing demands. For example, some of our people worked for global lines of service and had managers who were overseas and weren't aware of the work we were doing here in Australia. A lot of our employees were asking, 'How do I align my goals when people are making so many different demands of my time?'."

To answer this question the business created a simple goal alignment model that looked at the relationship between the demands of *My Company*, *My Business Unit* and *My Customer*. This model enabled employees to prioritise their goals and discuss competing stakeholder needs with their manager. The model clearly stated, *'customer-centric goals are your priority'*. McDonald adds, "We aligned our incentive plan around this model, ensuring customer priorities were given a larger proportion of the incentive."

Again, the business thrived under the *'customer intimacy'* vision and strategy. The most telling outcome was the number of re-bids the business won that year. By sheer coincidence, over 65 per cent of CSC's ongoing business contracts came up for renewal in 2006. Remarkably, the company won 12 out of 13 re-bids, an outstanding achievement.

The *Learning Map*® was refreshed for 2007 with the theme *Sailing with Success*. Again, it celebrated success, set the context for the journey and pointed everyone toward the final port of call, *'Customers Experience Results'*.

*"How do we consolidate and document
the learning materials and processes
so they are accessible?"*

The major focus for 2007 was horizontal alignment. McDonald explains, "We have cross-functional teams, called *Value Delivery Teams*, that come together from different lines of service to meet the needs of our customers. We had to make sure the people on these teams weren't more concerned about achieving the goals for their line of service than solving the customer problem that was sitting in front of them."

The challenge was to manage the tension between these competing demands. "To do this, we implemented *Value Delivery Team Goal Alignment Workshops*. These provided team members with a framework to surface any conflicts between customer requirements and business unit priorities. It's a way of managing the complex reality of our business; there's never a right or a wrong answer, it's about having a constructive conversation to make sure the needs of our customers and the business are both met."

McDonald explains how the business has developed a new incentive plan to entwine the goals of the people on these teams. "There's now a balancing act and an interlock between their incentive, where everyone shares the risk around revenue, costs and profit margin. Everyone now has an interest in making sure the team achieves its goals."

Looking ahead to the future, McDonald says the next step is working out how to move this from the status of strategic initiative, so it can endure once the resources and senior sponsorship end. "How do we consolidate and document the learning materials and processes so they are accessible? And how do we help our people know when they should use them?"

...this is a business that has undergone substantial change to realise its vision.

Goal alignment, vertical alignment, horizontal alignment — this is a business that has undergone substantial change to realise its vision. Has it been worth it? To answer this question, McDonald shares some of the improvements in performance that have occurred since the launch of the *'CSC Australia will be No.1 in Customer Intimacy'* vision.

On the employee front, engagement levels have soared over the period 2005–07. For example, there was a 10 percentage point increase in the number of employees who responded positively to the statement, 'I can see a connection between my work and CSC's mission and strategy'.

McDonald says the hard numbers provide further evidence that the *'customer intimacy'* vision and *'Get Aligned'* initiative are working. "The global business has three key financial metrics — revenue growth, operating income growth and return on invested capital. If you reach all three of these targets your business receives an *Eagle Award*. We've now won this award three years running, which is a global first at CSC."

The final accolade is that the global parent has noticed what is happening in Australia. They are now asking McDonald and the rest of the team at CSC to share some of their ideas and frameworks. Global alignment — now that's a challenge.

AMP

Leadership Frameworks

AMP is a leading wealth management company with more than 3.4 million customers and 3,500 employees in Australia and New Zealand. It is Australia's largest retail and corporate superannuation provider, and one of the region's most significant investment managers with more than $130 billion in assets under management.

What makes AMP's story particularly interesting is that it isn't just another run-of-the-mill corporate success story. In 2002 this venerable institution very nearly went to the wall. An ill-planned acquisition strategy led to the purchase of UK life insurance businesses that management clearly didn't understand. As the equities markets declined, AMP discovered it had to invest ever-increasing amounts of capital into its UK businesses to meet stringent regulatory requirements.

Over the course of 2002 the storm clouds gathered above AMP. As the size of the problem became apparent the market demanded action. The Board's response was to promote an insider, Andrew Mohl to the position of CEO and he immediately set about the task of saving this once great company.

Peter Gooding, HR Director at AMP recalls, "At that point we were in a pretty tough patch, the business was at real risk of going under. I can now look back and see it was leadership from the top that was key to our survival, because it reignited a core of people inside the business who could see what was going on and were horrified."

At this early stage in the recovery process, Mohl and his leadership team didn't adopt the inclusive style of leadership that is currently *'en vogue'*. "Leadership wasn't terribly collaborative; we didn't go around asking for people's opinions. Leaders were put into jobs to lead, make decisions and get on with it," says Gooding. "There was strong leadership, some really tough decisions made, but that's what needed to happen if the business was to survive."

Astutely, Mohl focused corporate head office on the core issues: de-merging the UK businesses, restoring the capital position of the company and regaining credibility with a disgruntled set of stakeholders — planners, clients and shareholders.

At the same time he established a new catchcry for the rest of the organisation, which was "Run the business better than it's been run before." This was an explicit challenge to everyone in the organisation to forget about the problems at the centre and instead focus on growing their market share and margins.

This was the first sign of a new loose/tight leadership approach emerging. As Gooding explains, "The management teams of our Australian businesses unencumbered by head office said, 'Gee we've got to do something', and they ran their businesses as hard as they could. We made sure they knew what was tight in the centre — values, strategy, objectives — but other than that they were given free rein to make things happen and they grabbed that opportunity with both hands."

As Mohl and his team began to pull the business back from the brink, the organisation moved into what Gooding describes as a transition stage. "The *'command-and-control'* approach had been appropriate for the time, but as we began to run the businesses more

"...it comes down to how well our leaders engage their people around what it is this business is trying to achieve."

effectively, as we righted our financial position and re-built our credibility in the market, we saw that this style of leadership wasn't going to work in the future."

This is where employee engagement entered the frame. Gooding's view is that in knowledge-based businesses like AMP, what you need to do is engage the hearts and minds of a really smart group of people to create new insights, new products and new opportunities. "It's the quality of having leadership that can extract this discretionary effort that sets a business apart. We drew this clear linkage between leadership and culture, where we knew that the single biggest leverage point for changing our culture was the leadership group and their behaviours."

During the transition, the leadership team adopted a transactional management style. They consulted with the business, but still made most of the decisions. "Now we've moved to a more adaptable leadership style where, when needed, we can say, 'no, this needs to be done this way', we can be collaborative and then we can be quite freethinking and empowering. It's a situational leadership model, and that's much more difficult for our leaders to use. This is why we need things like leadership frameworks."

To develop its leadership frameworks, AMP went back to basics to clarify what it is leaders really do, recalls Gooding. "We said, 'let's be clear about what leadership actually means'. Goal setting, coaching and delivering feedback are at the core of how we want our leaders to operate and we can't walk away from that. Basically, it comes down to how well our leaders engage their people around what it is this business is trying to achieve."

"...our ultimate aim was to lift the bench strength capability of our leadership right across the business."

Gooding explains that the leadership frameworks inside AMP are a set of skills and behaviours that everybody who is in a leadership position is expected to demonstrate. "To validate whether leaders are demonstrating these skills and behaviours, they all get assessed on their performance. The individual seeks input from their team, their peers and their boss. Ultimately, a report lands on their desk and they share the contents of that report with their staff and seek further input."

This was a challenge to begin with. There was a fear inside the business that this was a covert performance tool the leadership team would use to get rid of people. Gooding says, "We told them, 'no, the results from this report won't feature in your performance agreement, this is about your development'. We explained that our ultimate aim was to lift the bench strength capability of our leadership right across the business."

When AMP first ran the assessment program it brought in a large number of external coaches to help leaders interpret their reports and understand the sorts of conversations they needed to have with their colleagues. "It was coaching leaders on how to have brutally honest conversations around the key findings in their reports."

Gooding says the system delivers benefits on multiple levels. "At an organisational level we get quality reporting on what we're good at and what we're not so good at, as a group of leaders. The system also works at a team level, because you're sharing results and seeing what opportunities might exist for managers to engage more effectively with the business, their leader and their people. And it works at an individual level, as leaders and managers get the chance to extend their strengths and deal with their weaknesses."

The program initially started with the top 60–70 leaders. It is gradually being extended across the organisation and next year it is envisaged that all 800 leaders inside AMP will go through the assessment process. What most pleases Gooding is that the business is gradually building its coaching skills as it goes along. "We're weaning ourselves off external coaches to make sure that goal setting, coaching and delivering feedback are core skills that sit in everybody's leadership armoury."

The fact that AMP is comprised of two fundamentally different businesses made the introduction of the leadership frameworks into the organisation a particularly challenging assignment. One half of the business is AMP Financial Services; a distribution business that has a core suite of products and services and a distribution engine that feeds out through financial planners. The other half of the business is AMP Capital Investors; a product innovation business that is an active asset investment manager across multiple asset classes.

Each business took a distinct approach to the way it adopted the leadership frameworks. "AMP Capital Investors said, 'Right, we're an entrepreneurial business, we're about innovation'. They devised what they call a *Leadership Charter* around which they built their own assessment tool," says Gooding. "Over at AMP Financial Services, which is a bigger business in terms of the number of people, they implemented a similar system, but took a different approach, which they tagged *Sustainable Leadership*."

Gooding candidly admits that the larger of the businesses, AMP Financial Services had more of a problem culturally. "There was a socialised view of the way performance was rewarded. Everybody basically got the same reward and there weren't too many honest conversations about performance." To overcome this problem the business introduced a mandatory distribution curve that was all about comparative performance. Managers were told they had to make a ranking of the people on their team and that they would be held to account for the rankings they gave. The process was about using rewards to drive behavioural change and build a high performance culture inside the business.

Over at AMP Capital Investors they took a different approach. Its leadership team felt that adopting a mandatory curve wouldn't work. Instead, they relied on the markets to provide them with an absolute number against which they could calibrate performance. You beat the market and you got your reward; it was totally transparent. Again, adopting this reward system was about engaging minds, driving change and creating a culture within the business that would deliver results.

"Two different businesses, two different value drivers; so the leadership groups took two very different approaches to measuring and rewarding performance and they were both right," explains Gooding. "This is where we come back to the loose/tight approach, where everyone is clear about the things that we've all signed up for — like capital management, values and strategy — but outside of these the leadership group is free to run its part of the business as it sees fit."

"...people are prepared to give that discretionary effort which is fundamentally what engagement is all about."

To make this new performance system work, the leadership team needed to make sure that managers throughout the business used a less controlling leadership style. They too needed to become coaches, capable of having constructive conversations with their people regarding objectives, performance and reward.

Gooding says, "We're continuing to work with our managers in this area. We're helping them to understand how they can engage their people by asking them questions about possibilities and opportunities. To facilitate this we've set up something called a *Leadership and Culture* series, where panels of external leaders come in to give us their insights. We also run seminars and skill coaching sessions to really focus people around the essence of good quality goal setting, coaching and feedback."

The results are in, and AMP is seeing a steady rise in its engagement survey results. Interestingly, the organisation uses an internal survey, which makes benchmarking against similar organisations challenging. However, Gooding is keen to point out that the results have improved by 10 percentage points over the last three years. In addition, revenue and profits have steadily climbed, and the share price has regained much of its lost lustre.

What these results demonstrate is the importance of leadership in engaging the hearts and minds of a workforce. Gooding's view is, "Make sure that leaders are accountable and have the right skills, the right behaviours and the right values. If you get that dynamic right, the outcome is that people are prepared to give that discretionary effort which is fundamentally what engagement is all about."

VODAFONE AUSTRALIA

'Red, Rock Solid and Restless'

Vodafone Australia is a wholly owned subsidiary of the UK-based Vodafone Group PLC, the world's leading mobile communications group. Locally the business employs over 1,100 people, serves more than 3.7 million customers and holds an 18 per cent share of the mobile communications market. This is a substantial share, but it leaves the business positioned as a third-placed player to the market's 800-pound gorilla, Telstra.

Back in 2001 the local executive leadership team came to the conclusion that the only way Vodafone could successfully compete with its larger rivals was to connect and align every employee with the company's purpose, vision and values.

Vanessa Riley, Head of Career and Development at Vodafone Australia, recalls, "It was around this time that we started on our journey towards becoming a values-based organisation. We invested a lot of time and money into getting everyone in this business clear about what we stood for and where we were headed."

The business made headway over the ensuing years, steadily gaining market share and improving its performance. However, as with all journeys of this type, management knew it would be a mistake to set a course and slavishly stick to it. So, in 2005, the executive leadership team bunkered down to review its business strategy — with the aim of becoming a high performing values-based organisation.

"As part of the review, the executive leadership team began asking questions about the values we had in place at the time," explains Riley. "We were operating with separate *'people'* and *'brand'* values, and to be honest, we spent most of our time focusing on the

...a major employee engagement initiative aimed at bringing the essence of the Vodafone brand alive.

internal values. Many of our people struggled to even recall the external values, which of course meant we had a very internally focused culture."

By coincidence, at the same time that the Australian executive leadership team was reviewing its strategy, Vodafone Group in the United Kingdom was working on the global brand strategy. The outcome of this work was a major employee engagement initiative aimed at bringing the essence of the Vodafone brand alive. The focal point of this initiative was a new brand essence statement, *'Red, Rock Solid and Restless'*. This was a simple and memorable internal brand mantra designed to reinvigorate the culture of the business. *'Red'* symbolised passion and spirit, *'Rock Solid'* represented reliability and dependability, and *'Restless'* signified fresh thinking and innovation.

Riley notes, "In the end, it was a pretty simple decision for us to cull the existing values and replace them with *'Red, Rock Solid and Restless'*, which we in Australia saw as a set of values, as well the brand's essence."

The global brand team delegated the launch of *'Red, Rock Solid and Restless'* to the local markets. "They provided us with a framework that explained the thinking behind this new statement, but left it up to us to make it meaningful," explains Riley. "To launch the values we ran workshops for about 80 people at a time that unveiled the new values statement and explained its relationship to our new customer and people strategies."

Riley outlines the model used in these workshops — a clever combination of complexity and simplicity that established the relationship between *'Red, Rock Solid*

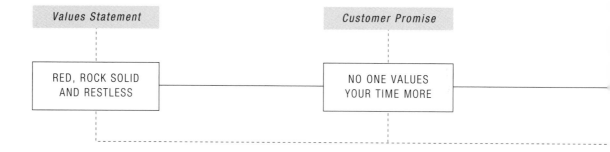

Values Statement		Customer Promise

RED, ROCK SOLID AND RESTLESS — NO ONE VALUES YOUR TIME MORE

and Restless' and the desired customer and employee experience. "Our goal was for our customers and our people to feel *'appreciated, confident and inspired'*. To do that we launched separate customer and people promises, which was a vital step because when you take it down to the level of making a promise, you get a greater sense of commitment from everyone."

Riley contines, "Our customer promise was, *'No one values your time more'*. That's what we believe; the commodity our customers value most is time, and if we can give them more time or help them to make better use of their time, that's where we can really add value. All our marketing now sits around this concept, which has evolved into our advertising line, *'Make the most of now'*.

"To deliver this customer promise, we knew we needed to make a similar offer to our people. Ultimately it's the people on the phones, in the stores and in the back office that have to bring our brand to life. The promise we wanted to make to them was, *'Be your possibility, make every moment count'* which took the same concept of valuing time, but looked at it from an employee's point of view."

Two promises were developed — one for customers and one for employees — both of which linked back to the externally and internally aligned values statement, *'Red, Rock Solid and Restless'*. This is a refreshingly simple framework that set out the future direction for the business. "It gave a clear signal to our people that we were starting on a new journey," says Riley.

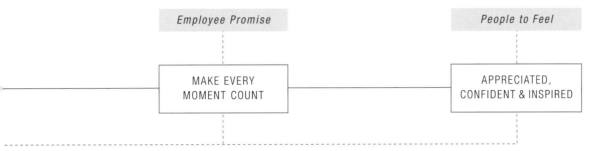

Employee Promise	People to Feel
MAKE EVERY MOMENT COUNT	APPRECIATED, CONFIDENT & INSPIRED

Running the workshops was only the beginning of the process. "We recognised that, '*Be your possibility...*' presented us with a huge opportunity in the engagement space," says Riley. "So we lined up all our employee touchpoints around this promise and began to develop individual propositions, that would address issues we knew were important to our people: things like career development, communication and recognition."

"Around this time we also started talking about the entire employee experience," explains Riley. "We realised we had to deliver something pretty special if we wanted our people, for instance, to turn down a great job offer from another company or do something that was above and beyond the call of duty."

This train of thought led to the development of Vodafone's Employee Value Proposition (EVP) — seven initiatives that represent the core of Vodafone Australia's people strategy and promise. "The EVP focuses on the emotional element of our people promise," says Riley. "We already had the rational side of our offer worked out, so this was about adding an emotional layer to help us build a more enduring connection with our people."

The scope of the program is so large that there is only space here to cover some of the highlights — *Welcomingyou, Lookingoutforyou* and *Celebratingyou.*

One of the most unique aspects of the *Welcomingyou* initiative is the focus given to the experience of new recruits during their first few hours inside the business. During this time many employees make a snap judgment as to whether their decision to join their new employer was the right one. Knowing this, Vodafone appointed a full-time Welcome

...a channel for leaders to promote the organisation's high performance, values-based culture...

Coordinator who, says Riley, "Meets you in reception as you arrive and presents you with your Vodafone backpack, which contains your mobile phone, your business cards, your laptop; in fact everything you need to start working. Then they take you to your desk, introduce you to your new colleagues and help you settle in." This is very different to the standard procedure in many companies, where new recruits are left to fend for themselves — an experience that can leave them feeling unwanted. By paying attention to the small details of the new recruits' first few hours in the job, there is a greater chance that they will reach the end of their first day feeling *'appreciated, confident and inspired'*.

The *Lookingoutforyou* initiative is another winner. There is an important functional side to this initiative that deals with health and safety issues, but it's the emotional side that is of most interest. This aspect of the initiative focuses on the wellbeing of employees and delivers a range of programs aimed at facilitating a healthy lifestyle. The goal of the initiative is to create happier, more resilient employees. "We offer fruit at work, 'flu vaccinations, massages, wellbeing seminars, health checks, flexible work policies: all sorts of things that go beyond the basic regulatory requirements," explains Riley. These benefits are increasingly important to younger workers, many of whom view them almost as a basic entitlement. Companies who refuse to offer these types of benefits will find it increasingly difficult to attract and retain talent in the future.

Formal and informal recognition is one of the big drivers of engagement. Over the last three years, Vodafone has developed a program that links employees' recognition to the company's business goals. The *Celebratingyou* initiative provides a channel for leaders to promote the organisation's high performance, values-based culture, by recognising and celebrating outstanding performance. The initiative has three levels of recognition:

- *Stars*: in-the-moment rewards, manager nominated
- *Heroes*: quarterly awards, manager nominated
- *Legends*: annual awards, employee nominated

Riley explains how each of these work. "*Stars* are our spontaneous rewards that leaders give out to recognise outstanding performance on a daily basis. There are various types of rewards, but generally they take the form of a $100 department store gift voucher that arrives on your desk with a thank you card from your leader saying, 'well done'."

Next are the *Heroes* awards. "These are quarterly events, where you celebrate the high performing people in your function. These awards come with a $500 gift that goes directly into your salary. But more importantly, the heroes get to go to somewhere fantastic for a day. For example, this year our heroes flew down to Perisher Blue in a private jet and spent the day skiing. It was a great reward, and it was something the entire business talked about," says Riley.

And the top awards, the annual *Legends* awards are peer nominated. "The winners are treated like rock stars, we give them the red carpet treatment from start to finish,"

"It's the way we treat our people... which ultimately determines the experience our customers get."

says Riley. "This year the *Legends* — and I think there were about 30 of them — went on holiday to Hawaii. It's a big expense, but recognising and celebrating outstanding effort is crucial if you want to build a high performance culture."

Vodafone Australia's EVP has helped the business to deliver on its people promises. As Riley notes, "It's the way we treat our people, the experience we give them while they're at work, which ultimately determines the experience our customers get. Our goal is to create an unbeatable experience for our people and our customers so they feel *'appreciated, confident and inspired'*."

Results across the business indicate that the brand, customer and people alignment efforts are paying off. In 2006–07 Vodafone Australia was recognised as a Hewitt Best Employer for the first time, achieving an overall engagement score of 76 per cent.[21] Vodafone's customers continue to experience the highest levels of customer satisfaction for mobile users in Australia.[22] And the financials are looking very healthy, with earnings growing by over 20 per cent year-on-year.[23]

ST GEORGE BANK

Workforce Capability

The St George Group's corporate strategy is one of differentiation based on people and customer experience. Turn to the St George Bank's annual report — you can download a copy at *www.stgeorge.com.au* — and you'll find a simple formula that the leadership team uses to drive this strategy.[24]

> engaged people + great customer experience = superior financial results

Well put. However, what's most striking about this formula is that it positions employee engagement at the top end of the strategy table. This is a business that clearly views its people and the culture in which they operate as a major competitive advantage. Sort out the people issues and everything else will follow.

If you look back at its history, this has always been part of the St George way — a focus on people and their relationships. This isn't marketing spin, or propaganda; this is a way of thinking and operating that pumps through the veins of this business. It makes sense that the leadership team has decided to leverage this particular strand of the bank's corporate DNA as part of its long-term strategy.

Peter Hall, Manager of People and Performance at St George Bank recalls that employee engagement has been a key focus for the bank since 2002. "We started on our *Best Bank* strategy at that time, and the framework that supported this demanded we build a high performance, team-based culture inside the business," he says. "This was all part of management's plan to differentiate the bank through engaged employees delivering great customer experiences."

The numbers demonstrate that this strategy is working. Over the past six years, the bank profits have soared from $376 million to $1,160 million, dividends have increased from 65 cents to 168 cents and total assets have grown from $52 billion to $125 billion.

To generate these results, St George has made substantial investments to develop the capability of its workforce. It has designed, developed and implemented a wide range of programs and initiatives aimed at building their skills and abilities.

A good example of this is the effort the bank has put into supporting the introduction of its *Local Market Model*. This is a strategy aimed at making local branch managers more responsive to their customers' needs. To execute this strategy, St George needed to provide its managers with training that would help them run their branches as small businesses. "We've given our branch managers a lot of business acumen training, helping them to develop their basic business skills so they can do things like read a balance sheet and understand the numbers inside their branch," says Hall. "And managers who are working inside this model now have more discretion to run their branch to better meet the needs of their local communities. Decisions that used to sit higher up are now theirs to take, which allows them to make smarter, faster decisions and deliver better service."

Many companies mistakenly overlook this part of the engagement equation. Providing people with the skills, resources and space they need to do their work is a powerful driver

Many companies mistakenly overlook this part of the engagement equation.

of engagement; it empowers them, which in turn helps them to find a way of generating discretionary effort on a daily basis.

St George has introduced a number of other initiatives aimed at enhancing the bank's already solid reputation for customer service. One area of focus has been the bank's induction program for customer service officers. The Human Resources team has developed a program that provides new recruits with the information and tools they need to perform to the expected high standards of the company. As Hall explains, "Every customer service officer who joins us goes through a three-week induction program before they join their branch. Then they go into the workplace to gain some experience, before returning for one more week of training. This training means these people can go out into a branch and immediately make a difference, which works for them and works for our customers."

The training doesn't stop once the new recruits are onboard. Hall explains that the bank offers a combination of classroom and online learning, delivered through St George's innovative e-learning system, *e-luminate*. The online learning programs offer short, sharp bursts of training that last no more than 20 minutes.

"We've recently enhanced this system with the introduction of another tool, *Smart Job Guides*. Rather than a 20-minute course, it's a quick two- or three-minute course that tells you, for example, how to use the particular part of the system you're in," says Hall. "The idea is based on workflow learning, which aims to integrate learning into the workplace

Attempting to satisfy and engage a workforce that contains workers from three different generations is always going to be difficult.

rather than having it as something separate. The guides are easily accessible, so when someone wants to know how to do something, the information is there for them to use."

This is clever stuff that delivers benefits on many levels. It enables customer service officers to deliver a superior service to customers, which aligns with the bank's core strategy. It also ensures the workforce doesn't drown in information.

As Hall astutely notes, "Information is a double-edged sword: our people need it, but give them too much and they become overwhelmed. These *Smart Job Guides* allow our people to learn what they need to learn, when they need to learn it. And even more importantly, it gives our people a greater sense of control over their work, which is an incredibly important benefit. There is nothing more stressful — or disengaging — than being asked to undertake a task that you have neither the knowledge nor the skills to successfully complete."

Most businesses in Australia will not have the resources to implement a learning solution that matches the one described here. But that's not the point. Every leadership team, no matter what size of business they are running, needs to make sure that their people have the information, training and tools they need to do their work.

Hall, who has just returned from the Human Resources team's annual conference, explains where the bank's thinking on the issue of employee engagement is heading. "We're moving towards a model where we're going to do more about managing individuality. If you look at the work that everybody does around engagement, it tends to be very homogeneous. You eventually get to a point where you've done everything the survey is telling you to do, so you need to start doing something different."

Hall says St George's idea is to look at the issue through a generational lens. "If you believe only a third of the stuff around generational differences, in terms of what people at different stages of their lives want from their employer and from their work, it tells you that you can't treat everybody in exactly the same way."

This is an interesting perspective and it feels right. Attempting to satisfy and engage a workforce that contains workers from three different generations is always going to be difficult. Managers shouldn't approach this task with the expectation that a one-size-fits-all solution is going to work. As Hall notes, "How do you manage and lead someone who's 58? It can't be the same way as you handle someone who's 24. It's a real challenge to keep them both happy, but that's the challenge we need to meet."

St George has already made progress in this area with its industry-leading range of staff benefits. At one end of the generational scale the bank offers new parents 13 weeks of paid leave. At the other end, the bank recently introduced a program that allows more mature staff to take 12 months of flexible unpaid leave to care for grandchildren. It's the ability to offer employees this degree of flexibility that will set apart employers of choice in the future. But as Hall notes, "This is just the start of what we need to do. It's the benefits piece. The next part is the difficult bit, trying to tailor the employment experience to the wants and needs of the individual."

...what currently passes as best practice isn't going to cut it in the future.

Hall says the move towards this individual engagement concept will require the Human Resources team to develop programs and courses that help the bank's managers to identify the needs and preferences of the individuals on their team. "We need to give our managers the tools and training to do this, so they can have more meaningful conversations with their people, as this is really how engagement is built."

These comments paint a much more complex picture of the future. Hall is telling us that what currently passes as best practice isn't going to cut it in the future. The programs St George has put in place over the last six or so years have allowed it to grab the low-hanging fruit. Staff turnover has fallen by 15 per cent and staff satisfaction has soared from 48 per cent to 75 per cent. However, to improve on these results the bank will need to implement what we might term *Employee Engagement 2.0*: the next phase in the management of human capital where the *'people and relationship'* skills of individual managers dictate an organisation's engagement score.

Developing a workforce that has a strong capability in this area is the ultimate challenge. As Hall says, "We can no longer treat everyone the same way, so we need to build the employment experience around the individual. To do that we have to get our managers to understand their role in this."

MALLESONS STEPHEN JAQUES

Mentoring Program

Mallesons Stephen Jaques is Australia's leading law firm and one of Asia's largest and most influential. The firm's annual revenue is almost $500 million, but what's more striking is that the firm grew its revenue line by over 16 per cent in 2006–07. This is an outstanding achievement in what is widely acknowledged to be a highly competitive legal market. What is the secret to Mallesons' success?

Kate Rimer, Executive Director of People and Development at Mallesons, reveals that the foundations for this success were laid in 2004 with the appointment of Robert Milliner as Chief Executive Partner. "Robert really wanted to revisit the firm's entire strategy, short- and long-term," says Rimer. "It was about asking simple questions such as: 'Where is the growth going to come from?' and 'Where is the profit going to come from?'"

Rimer believes this review of the firm's strategy provided the ideal platform for the P&D team's subsequent engagement efforts. "Our work in this area started with a business need and competitive pressure, not HR getting enthusiastic about a whole raft of initiatives they wanted to push into the business."

While Milliner worked collaboratively with the partners to establish the future direction of the business, Rimer's team looked at the firm's *People & Development* strategy. "We intuitively felt certain things needed to happen. We needed to bring people together. We needed to throw open the doors on communication. Our Chief Executive wanted to get back to the fundamentals of developing people. Yes, there were already great training programs in place, but we needed to look at opportunities such as mentoring, where for a small investment you get a big return. We saw it as getting back to the basics of what makes a high performance culture work and how you get engagement."

As these ideas began to take shape, the firm made plans for its first employee opinion survey, the *Vibe*. Mallesons selected Towers Perrin-ISR to conduct the survey, attracted by the comparative norms that would allow the firm to benchmark its performance against other global professional services firms and Australian organisations.

As Rimer talks about the firm's first survey, she shares an interesting insight. "It's important," she says, "that you manage the expectations of people who are going through this process for the first time. When we launched the survey, we made it clear to the partners that the first year's results wouldn't be that important. Their response was, 'What do you mean? We're all going to be waiting for them.' I said, 'No, it's the year after and the year after that which are important, because then we'll begin to see trends and we can track progress.' When the results did arrive, everyone understood the context in which they were looking at them — to make plans for the year ahead."

Pleasingly, the firm achieved a participation rate of 76 per cent for its first survey. Rimer says, "This gave us a huge mandate for change, because we knew three-quarters of our partners and staff wanted certain things."

The findings from the survey threw the spotlight on the standard themes that required attention: partner leadership, performance management, flexibility and diversity, training, remuneration and benefits, career development and communication.

"When we launched the survey, we made it clear to the partners that the first year's results wouldn't be that important."

The firm set to work implementing a wide range of programs and interventions aimed at addressing specific problem areas. "One particular issue that came out of the survey was mentoring," recalls Rimer. "People felt they weren't getting enough of it in the firm; they wanted more opportunities for communication and development."

The firm's response was to design and develop the *Mallesons Mentoring* program — an informal opt-in support system for all staff. The rationale behind the program was for a more experienced member of staff to pair up with a less experienced colleague to support their personal and professional development.

"To start the program we opened up a database and said, 'If you want a mentor or want to become a mentor, register'. As people began to sign up we used the HR people on the ground in each city to match them up," Rimer explains.

"We then ran *Learning Express Workshops*, which were quick 30-minute workshops that explained the basic concepts that lie behind mentoring, laid down some boundaries for people to work with and basically encouraged everyone to give it a go."

The program commenced in February 2005 with over 630 partners, legal, shared services and support staff participating — nearly a third of the workforce. The aim was that everyone who signed up for the program would benefit in some way. On one side of the relationship, the mentees would get access to a *'sounding board'*, advice on how to tackle work challenges, tips on how to achieve work-life balance and the opportunity to broaden their network in the firm. On the other side, the mentors would get the chance

Feedback like this explains how a mentoring program can help to drive engagement.

to develop their leadership capabilities, practise their listening and communication skills, and gain access to the opinions of other people inside the firm.

Rimer's own experience with the program is a good example of how it works in practice. "I'm mentored by a senior partner who used to be chairman of the firm and she's brilliant. She was the first partner of the firm to take maternity leave and work part-time so she always has invaluable advice to share with me as a working mum. Then I mentor our head of security who's never worked in a law firm before, so it's an interesting chain — I learn about the firm's culture from my mentor and I can then share that knowledge with my mentee."

One of the perennial challenges with this type of program is keeping it at the top of people's minds. Rimer mentions two tools her team uses to do this.

"A couple of times a year we promote our *Macchiato Moments* program, where we offer mentors a voucher for the coffee shop in their building and encourage them to go for a coffee with the person they're mentoring."

"We've also introduced a *Chief Executive's Mentoring Award*, where people in each city nominate other participants for an award. It's another way for us to promote the program and recognise and reward those people who are participating in it."

The program is clearly working. Three years in and the number of participants registered in the program has increased to 660, which suggests that people are getting a lot more out of it than a free coffee.

At this point Rimer shares some internal research that provides feedback from participants. The unattributed quotes are particularly heartening. For example:

"It has been an absolute godsend at times. It's very informal and just gives me that additional avenue to discuss work and non-work issues outside of my group and people I usually work with. I have truly benefited from the calming, wise advice I am given — sometimes just saying the problem out loud helps — so it's nice to have that available."

And

"I couldn't have asked for a better mentor. He's not just a mentor; he's a friend and life coach and takes a genuine interest in what is happening in my life outside work too. It's changed my whole perception of working at the firm…"

Feedback like this explains how a mentoring program can help to drive engagement. It provides people with an easier way to resolve day-to-day problems, which leaves them feeling accomplished. It enables the mentee to draw on the experience of their mentor, so they can work more efficiently. And it assists in propagating the firm's culture, which helps people — especially new recruits — to feel that they belong.

The numbers from the *Vibe* survey over the last four years indicate that the program is having the desired impact. The affirmative response to the following statement: 'I have access to the mentoring and/or coaching (formal and informal) I need.' has risen from 60 per cent in 2004, to a more pleasing 77 per cent in 2007. This is a very impressive 14 percentage points above the Towers Perrin-ISR *Global Professional Services Norm*.

The survey's participation rate has also shot up. Rimer says, "It's now at 89 per cent and given that 10 per cent of the firm is on leave at any one time, we don't think we'll get much higher than that. What's so exciting about this increase is that people will only fill in the survey if they think you're listening, and they only know you're listening if they see you doing something about issues they've highlighted."

The firm's partners are another group who are embracing the survey. Rimer explains, "We now have partners asking for the report for their practice team, their city, or their centre. It's demand-driven rather than us pushing it out there. They're saying, 'Where's my report?' 'I want to know what the issues are' 'I want to sit down with HR and talk about how can we build a plan' and so on."

Interestingly, the firm doesn't talk about an overall engagement score, preferring instead to focus attention on performance in discrete categories. For example, the firm's *Collaboration and Teamwork* score sits at a massive 17 percentage points above the Towers Perrin-ISR *Australian National Norm*. And this year's *Partner Leadership* score showed a dramatic 8 percentage point improvement over last year's figure.

Focusing on performance in discrete categories isn't an approach that is unique to Mallesons, but there is a feeling that this firm is more concerned than most about focusing on individual drivers of engagement. The firm's leadership knows if they can get the individual parts of their program working, above-average performance across a wide range of metrics is almost certain to follow.

"We now have partners asking for the report for their practice team, their city, or their centre."

Rimer also points out that the mentoring bug is taking hold at the firm. "There's an informal mums' network that's started in Sydney and Melbourne for female partners and senior associates who get together for lunch every month. Conversations are starting with, 'What do you do with your clients on the days you're not in the office?' or 'How do you manage your BlackBerry?' or 'Where are you sending your children for childcare?' The mentoring that is happening at those lunches is fantastic."

Rimer wraps up by saying, "If you can get a community of people to come together there's not much they can't solve, as they have all the ideas and support they need within the group." It's a well-made point, and explains why every organisation that wants to drive up engagement levels should consider setting up a mentoring program.

CHAPTER 9

Hints and Tips

Although each engagement expedition is unique, there are always marked similarities among the problems and issues that crop up. Knowing the pitfalls and developing strategies to overcome them can help the team navigate their chosen route.

Tip #01: Get the boss on board. If the engagement team doesn't have the unequivocal support of the CEO it may as well disband. Setting up and running an engagement program always entails substantial change. If the CEO isn't supportive of this change, in fact if he or she isn't driving it, the program will fail.

Tip #02: Address a broad range of issues. Often, it is a single issue — for example, workforce retention — that pushes employee engagement onto management's agenda. Once there, executives should broaden their perspective and look at what other problems they can tackle. A carefully thought through initiative can deal with issues that reach far beyond the standard themes of employee attraction and retention. Difficulties with executing strategy, declining quality levels and customer service breakdowns are all examples of problems management can resolve with their engagement program.

Tip #03: Get the basics sorted. Before executives can start building their employees' engagement levels, they need to sort out the fundamentals that underpin their business. Employee engagement is not, and never will be, an alternative to a strong leadership team

Generating intellectual and emotional buy-in requires something more substantial than an email from the CEO.

with a clear vision and a winning strategy. For example, attempting to create alignment around a flawed corporate plan will only hasten the slide in an organisation's already disappointing engagement scores. Newly appointed leaders who want to effect rapid change can find this frustrating. They want to re-energise and refocus their workforce, but they should slow down. They need the basics in position — purpose, vision, values, objectives, strategy and priorities — before they can attempt to reshape the attitudes and behaviours of their employees.

Tip #04: Don't impose the program from above. Executives who attempt to impose their will on their workforce almost always meet strong resistance. Employees want to know what is happening and why, before they'll commit themselves to a particular course of action. Generating intellectual and emotional buy-in requires something more substantial than an email from the CEO. The leadership team needs to take the entire workforce on a journey, explaining to them why the program is necessary, how it will affect them and what they can expect to gain from it.

Tip #05: Encourage employees to voice their concerns. Employees sometimes feel threatened by the prospect of change. Forced to leave behind the trusted and familiar, they withhold their commitment or worse, sabotage the initiative. To prevent this, the team needs to open a dialogue that encourages employees to voice their concerns.

Employee engagement is not a quick-fix solution to what are, typically, deeply entrenched systemic problems.

Executives cannot afford to be casual with the truth during these discussions. If the program is to coincide with job cuts, the workforce needs to know this upfront. Covering up bad news only makes its impact more devastating when it does occur. An open, honest conversation generates trust and respect. If employees can see the logic and fairness behind a decision, they'll be more likely to support it.

Tip #06: Don't view engagement as a quick-fix. Throughout this book, the terms *'program'*, *'project'* and *'initiative'* have been used interchangeably. This is potentially quite misleading. Employee engagement is not a quick-fix solution to what are, typically, deeply entrenched systemic problems. Referring to this work as an initiative implies there is a timeframe within which the entire workforce will become engaged, at which point everyone can move onto other tasks. Of course this never happens. All the benefits that quick-fix solutions deliver disappear as quickly as they arrived. Executives need to prepare themselves for at least 12–24 months of hard work before they begin to see signs of substantial improvement. And it can take up to four years for the full set of promised benefits to make their appearance.

Tip #07: Be prepared for a substantial bill. Generating employee understanding and commitment requires a substantial investment of time and money. These are both scarce resources, so before the team moves into launch mode it needs to realistically estimate the funds it requires to run the program. If the program is taking place inside a business that employs thousands of workers and the schedule of work includes the introduction of new technology platforms and staff retraining, management can be looking at a price tag that runs into the millions of dollars. Readers who are shaking their heads in disbelief should know that one large resources company spent over $30 million on its engagement program. However, these numbers shouldn't discourage executives of smaller companies. Budgets that are a tiny fraction of this in size can still generate outstanding results.

Tip #08: Identify what is impeding engagement. The team needs to break down the barriers to engagement before it can start to build the bridges. Examples of these barriers include a communication system that sends out mixed messages, internal policies that hinder rather than help, and reward systems that drive the wrong sorts of behaviours. Qualitative and quantitative research studies can help management to identify the obstacles to engagement that exist inside their organisation.

Tip #09: Give people the space to work it out for themselves. Engagement strategies can become too prescriptive. The engagement team gets to work and before they know it they've created a new suite of HR policies that are more authoritarian than the ones they replaced. Instead of falling into this trap, the team should look for ways of encouraging employees to take ownership of their own career path and development plan. Encouraging people to make decisions for themselves, whether designing their job or deciding on their quarterly targets, generates involvement and commitment. Don't attempt to solve every problem with a new rule or regulation. Allow some space for people to work it out for themselves.

Tip #10: Help employees to understand the numbers. Most employees have little or no understanding of the numbers that determine financial performance. Even at the top of the pyramid, senior executives often have no idea of the basics, such as the cost of the capital they are using. To successfully engage a workforce, management needs to make sure everyone knows the rules of the game. What are the financial drivers of this business? What key ratios or numbers most tellingly reveal performance? How do you calculate these ratios or numbers? What causes them to shift? Drilling this information into the business helps focus everyone's efforts onto moving the numbers that matter.

Tip #11: Use business jargon very sparingly. The indiscriminate use of business jargon can discourage employees from participating in and committing to an engagement program. *'Friction margins'* and *'market-based management'* are just two examples of the terminology executives love to use, but which employees find difficult to understand, or worse, alienating. Even the use of seemingly innocuous phrases like *'employee engagement'* can cause misunderstanding. "What are they trying to do to us now?" say

Drilling this information into the business helps focus everyone's efforts onto moving the numbers that matter.

alarmed workers, when they first hear that senior executives are planning to lift workforce engagement levels. Executives need to simplify their written and verbal communication, so messages can get through to the workforce without being misinterpreted. If practical, the engagement team should pre-test their messages with a representative sample of the workforce to ensure they can comprehend the communication. The trick is to not *'dumb down'* the messages so far that they begin to lose impact or meaning. To borrow a phrase from Einstein, "Things should be made as simple as possible, and no simpler."

Tip #12: Push the program out into the business. To generate lasting success, the engagement team needs to push ownership of the program into every corner of the business. The executives at the centre of the engagement program should have the long-term goal of relinquishing control of their initiatives. At some point, the workforce needs to take over and this needs to happen sooner rather than later. The best solution is to actively engineer the program into the framework of the business. Using this approach encourages employees to view these initiatives as a permanent fixture in their lives, rather than a one-off event.

Tip #13: Consider your plan of attack. There exists a school of thought that suggests executives shouldn't attempt to launch too many initiatives at once, based on the belief that employees have a finite ability to cope with change. This is an important aspect to be

There is a tendency for senior executives to think of employee engagement as a rank and file issue.

aware of and, in tandem with the universal problem of limited resources, it might appear management's wisest course of action is to focus their attention on a few select projects at a time. However, breaking through cultural inertia may require a more holistic approach. For example, which of these initiatives should the team exclude from their plans?

- Sacrifice the deployment of a robust measurement system?
- Bypass the development of an effective internal communication system?
- Or, cancel the implementation of a customer service training program?

Each of these initiatives is important and to omit any one of them might undermine the effectiveness of the entire program. Consequently, some executives who have been down this path suggest that the best strategy is to move forward on all fronts — though noting it is necessary to break the program down into manageable parts. It's the most challenging and costly approach to adopt, but it offers the best chance of success.

Tip #14: Start work at the top of the pyramid. There is a tendency for senior executives to think of employee engagement as a rank and file issue. They start their work at the bottom of the organisational pyramid believing they can tackle the leadership team at a later date. This is the wrong call. There is no point in commencing a dialogue with employees about their attitudes and behaviour, if those employees are going to see their leaders operating outside of the mandated behavioural boundaries. The engagement team should commence their work at the very top of the organisation. These people set the tone for everyone else. As a rule, programs should cascade down through a business, from the leadership team to senior managers, from senior managers to team leaders, from team leaders to team members.

Tip #15: Test-market initiatives first. Where possible, executives should trial major initiatives before they commit to a full launch. The deployment of a poorly designed intervention can create a negative perception that irreparably damages the program. Take, for example, the introduction of team huddles. This widely used communication tool can generate discord if workers view it as an unnecessary interruption to their already busy day. Testing the huddles in one or two locations gives everyone the chance to see what is and isn't working. Team leaders get the chance to shape the agenda. Team members get the opportunity to say what does and doesn't work for them. And the program's architects get to see what impact the huddle has on performance. Eight weeks later the engagement team can confidently launch a tried and tested initiative.

Tip #16: Use different strokes for different folks. Rarely will a single engagement strategy work for everyone. For example, consider the workforce inside a large retailer. The engagement drivers for a junior sales assistant and a senior buyer are typically very different. If an engagement program is to succeed, it needs to account for these differences. Coding the quantitative survey responses enables the research company to identify the drivers for specific groups of employees. By referring to the codes, the research company can isolate the engagement drivers by job type, position, tenure, age and so on. This information enables the engagement team to develop targeted strategies for discrete groups of workers.

Tip #17: Recognise that cultures are rarely homogeneous. Building on the above theme, the engagement team also needs to be cognisant of the fact that corporate cultures are rarely homogeneous. Different divisions and departments will all have a distinctive culture, which probably means the engagement program needs to take a different approach inside each of these operating units. In most instances, it is beneficial if the results from the engagement survey flow down to the workforce. The granulation of the research results by division, department and team, allows these groups to identify and address specific issues inside their operating unit.

Top #18: Work small to get the best results. The level at which an engagement team launches its interventions often determines the success of the program. Launching a program into a division or department is a difficult task. The sheer size of the group can dilute any sense of ownership — everyone believes someone else is responsible. It can

This information enables the engagement team to develop targeted strategies for discrete groups of workers.

be more effective to deploy interventions within smaller work groups, no bigger in size than 12–15 people. Inside these groups it's far more likely that the team leader and the team will take ownership of the initiative.

Tip #19: Reinforce key messages at the outset. At the beginning of the program, the engagement team needs to regularly communicate with the rest of the business. A comprehensive communication program built around objectives, strategies and results will provide employees with a clear view of what is happening, and why. As the program progresses the volume dial can be turned down, but at the outset, the louder the better.

Tip #20: Use praise to embed in new behaviours. Some managers have a propensity to spend their day reprimanding employees. This constant criticism poisons the climate inside a group, an outcome that adversely affects productivity and profitability. To overcome this problem, managers need to learn how to use formal and informal recognition techniques to motivate and manage their people. Praise, and lots of it, is the key to wiring new behaviours into the organisation.

Tip #21: Be prepared for some dark days. On this type of journey the climate inside a business often takes a dramatic turn for the worse before it begins to improve. The list of changed conditions workers have to contend with is long — a revised ideology, new

It is a mistake to overlook the importance of traditional HR skills to the success of the program.

corporate strategy, modified operating systems, reworked reporting lines. Workers often struggle with the transition and many become frustrated with the rapid pace of change. This is when the engagement program is at its most vulnerable. Critics will swoop on any decline in morale and performance as evidence of the program's shortcomings. The engagement team needs to head off these attacks by predicting them and putting in place initiatives — regular celebratory events for example — to assuage their effects.

Tip #22: Consult with employees over major decisions. Everything is going well. Engagement scores are rising, customer satisfaction figures are trending in the right direction and, most pleasingly, revenue is growing. Then — without warning — the business announces it is transferring part of its back-office operations to the sub-continent. Employees are shocked and more than a little angry. In the next survey all the lead indicators are heading south, and it is safe to assume the profit figure is set to follow. This is disappointing. Why do engagement levels often plunge at the first sign of adversity? It boils down to an issue of trust. Employees are no longer prepared to put up with decisions that deliver benefits to shareholders — especially senior executives who hold stock — and pain to everyone else. If the leadership team wants to maintain high levels of engagement, it needs to start consulting with employees over major business decisions. These consultations should take place, if at all possible, in advance of the news going public, and senior executives should try to listen more than they talk.

Tip #23: Use traditional HR skills. It is a mistake to overlook the importance of traditional HR skills to the success of the program. Meticulous recruitment systems, innovative remuneration policies and effective performance management programs are the bedrock of employee engagement.

Tip #24: Don't let consultants run the entire program. It is also a mistake to place an engagement program in the hands of external consultants. While consultants can provide valuable advice and assistance, they should play a support role, not a starring one. A sustainable improvement in engagement levels only occurs if line managers and employees can see the role they have to play in securing the success of the program. If consultants take charge of the program, the majority of the workforce will see it as someone else's responsibility — a mindset that will condemn the initiative to failure.

Tip #25: Provide employees with a roadmap to their future. Employees who can see a future for themselves inside a business are far more engaged than those who cannot. Every employee needs a personal and professional development plan that acts as his or her roadmap to the future. What skills, knowledge and experience do they need to acquire so they can reach their potential? This isn't solely about making plans to take the next step up the corporate ladder. It's more about making sure everyone in the business has the opportunity to learn, develop, grow and achieve.

CONCLUSION

Attraction, Retention and Productivity

The challenges that are pushing employee engagement onto management's radar aren't going to disappear. Skills shortages are worsening, workforce expectations are increasing and shareholders are demanding an ever-higher rate of return on their investment.

The firms that I spoke to, when writing this book, foresaw all of this a number of years ago and decided to act. Thanks to their efforts, we now have the evidence to demonstrate that employee engagement offers a solution to these challenges. By taking a *'people-first'* approach to managing their operations, these companies have been able to grow their headcount, satisfy the demands of their people and lift productivity.

Attraction, retention and, most importantly, productivity — these are the keys that open the door to employee engagement. Few leaders decide to invest time and money into this area for purely altruistic reasons; they go down this path because the numbers stack up. The link between *'people, performance and profits'* has become undeniable.

Indeed, it was this link that first attracted me to the topic of employee engagement over five years ago. When I began researching this book three years ago, I already had in place the roadmap that lies at the heart of this book. Pleasingly, my conversations with the executives I interviewed confirmed the relevance of the roadmap and the thinking that underpinned it.

However, in these conversations a number of points kept cropping up. I'd like to conclude this book by stating these points, as I believe they highlight the opportunities that lie ahead of those who are about to set out on an engagement journey.

...these companies have been able to grow their headcount, satisfy the demands of their people and lift productivity.

The first point, and it's perhaps obvious, is that employee engagement is much more than an attraction and retention tool. A few years ago, many engagement programs stopped at the stage of developing a compelling employee value proposition. Now this work only gets you a ticket to the game. The real challenge with employee engagement is getting a workforce to focus on the task of successfully executing a corporate strategy.

Second, the companies who have been doing this work for five or more years have managed to align their corporate, people and engagement strategies. Achieving this level of integration is crucial if the engagement program is to impact the bottom line. It takes clarity of thinking to initially establish the links, but once formed, they ensure that every action is directed towards achieving a single goal.

Third, the circuit breaker on engagement is always leadership behaviour. If the people at the top aren't *'walking the talk'* then the program will fail to gain traction. In fact, one of the executives I interviewed said the biggest challenge was getting the leadership team to understand that *'they'* were the problem. The situation only improves if the leadership team accepts that the change process needs to commence with them.

Fourth, a number of firms I spoke to are shifting their focus away from large-scale engagement interventions. These firms have already lifted their employees' engagement levels to industry-leading levels and are now searching for ways to drive it even higher. To achieve this goal they are looking at the relationship between team leader and team member, as it is here that engagement is most commonly developed or destroyed.

The insight here is: businesses
don't change, people do.

Fifth, executives who have worked long and hard at lifting internal engagement levels universally want to embed the engagement program into the framework of their business. While it retains the status of initiative there is the real risk that when the program's sponsors and supporters move on, new management will look at the entire exercise as an unnecessary expense. To preclude this, they are hard-wiring key interventions into the business so they become standard operating procedure.

Sixth, companies that are really shifting the needle on this issue are generating engagement by helping employees to undergo a personal transformation. The insight here is: businesses don't change, people do. Helping people to understand the seeds of their behaviour and providing them with mechanisms to manage their relationships with others is an extremely effective way of driving engagement.

Ultimately, what I have discovered is that a well-designed engagement strategy takes into account the deep and complex roots of employee satisfaction, commitment and motivation. It doesn't paper over the cracks with shallow and simplistic solutions; it goes back to basics and rebuilds the employer-employee relationship from the ground up. Companies that do this — and engage their employees around the task of executing the corporate strategy — can look forward to the prospect of higher revenues and profits.